Education

Printed for
Remnant Publications
by
Pacific Press Publishing Association
Boise, Idaho
Oshawa, Ontario, Canada

Cover art by Harry Anderson

This edition published 1995

Printed in the United States of America

ISBN 1-883012-66-X

The bracketed numbers at the foot of each page co-ordinate this edition with the pagination of the standard hardback printings.

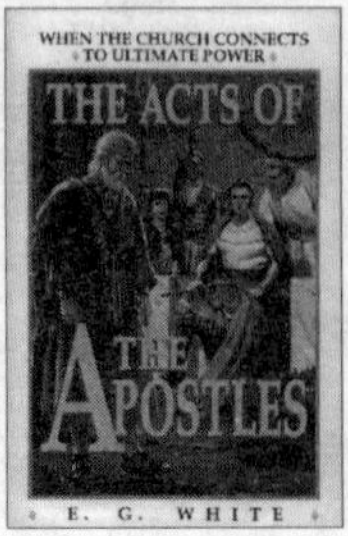

What makes this set so popular? The Results!

Lifechanging Results

The Bible Study Companion Set *$39.75

All five books together covering Genesis to Revelation — from the beginning of the universe through human history and on into our future. This set truly enriches your life with a better

Patriarchs and Prophets

Where did the human race come from? Why do bad things happen to good people? Why are babies born sick, and why do so many hard-working people never seem to get ahead? If God is good, why doesn't He prevent sadness and heartbreak? And if He is all-powerful, why doesn't He do something about evil and sickness? These questions and many more are answered in this remarkable book. Patriarchs and Prophets has brought peace and hope to millions throughout the world. *US$7.95

Prophets and Kings

Beginning with King Solomon, this book recounts the stories of great men and women of the Bible who lived from his reign to the first advent of Jesus Christ. Here you will read of Elijah, Daniel, Isaiah, and Jeremiah, among others–and you will find the lessons God would have us all learn from their lives. *US$7.95

The Desire of Ages

This book is about the Man who stands at the center of all human history. No one else has had such a profound influence on the people of this planet as Jesus Christ. *US$7.95

The Acts of the Apostles

This book is about power–ultimate power. The awesome power of the Holy Spirit, and what He can do in human lives when we surrender to be used by Him. When Pentecost came upon the early church, what God's people accomplished was miraculous. And all that the apostles did, God wants to do again through us today. *US$7.95

The Great Controversy

The world is on the verge of a stupendous crisis. Here is the authoritative answer to the confusion and despair of this tense age. Revealing God's ultimate plan for mankind, The Great Controversy may be the most important book you'll ever read. *US$7.95

Contents

First Principles

Illustrations

The Master Teacher

Nature Teaching

The Bible as an Educator

Physical Culture

Character Building

The Underteacher

The Higher Course

First Principles

"We all, with unveiled face reflecting as a mirror the glory of the Lord, are transformed into the same image from glory to glory."

1
Source and Aim of True Education

"The knowledge of the holy is understanding;" "Acquaint now thyself with Him."

Our ideas of education take too narrow and too low a range. There is need of a broader scope, a higher aim. True education means more than the pursual of a certain course of study. It means more than a preparation for the life that now is. It has to do with the whole being, and with the whole period of existence possible to man. It is the harmonious development of the physical, the mental, and the spiritual powers. It prepares the student for the joy of service in this world and for the higher joy of wider service in the world to come.

The source of such an education is brought to view in these words of Holy Writ, pointing to the Infinite One: In Him "are hid all the treasures of wisdom." Colossians 2:3. "He hath counsel and understanding." Job 12:13.

The world has had its great teachers, men of giant intellect and extensive research, men whose utterances have stimulated thought and opened to view vast fields of knowledge; and these men have been honored as guides and benefactors of their race; but there is One who stands higher than they. We can trace the line of the world's teachers as far back as human records extend; but the Light was before them. As the moon and the stars of our solar system shine by the reflected light of the sun, so, as far as their teaching is true, do the world's great thinkers reflect the rays of the Sun of Righteousness. Every gleam of thought, every flash of the intellect, is from the Light of the world.

In these days much is said concerning the nature and importance of "higher education." The true "higher education" is that imparted by Him with whom "is wisdom and strength" (Job 12:13), out of whose mouth "cometh knowledge and understanding." Proverbs 2:6.

In a knowledge of God all true knowledge and real development have their source. Wherever we turn, in the physical, the mental, or the spiritual realm; in whatever we behold, apart from the blight of sin, this knowledge is revealed. Whatever line of investigation we pursue, with a sincere purpose to arrive at truth, we are brought in touch with the unseen, mighty Intelligence that is working in and through all. The mind of man is brought into communion with the mind of God, the finite with the Infinite. The effect of such communion on body and mind and soul is beyond estimate.

In this communion is found the highest education. It is God's own method of development. "Acquaint now thyself with Him" (Job 22:21), is His message to mankind. The method outlined in these words was the method followed in the education of the father of our race. When in the glory of sinless manhood Adam stood in holy Eden, it was thus that God instructed him.

In order to understand what is comprehended in the work of education, we need to consider both the nature of man and the purpose of God in creating him. We need to consider also the change in man's condition through the coming in of a knowledge of evil, and God's plan for still fulfilling His glorious purpose in the education of the human race.

When Adam came from the Creator's hand, he bore, in his physical, mental, and spiritual nature, a likeness to his Maker. "God created man in His own image" (Genesis 1:27), and it was His purpose that the longer man lived the more fully he should reveal this image—the more fully reflect the glory of the Creator. All his faculties were capable of development; their capacity and vigor were continually to increase. Vast was the scope offered for their exercise, glorious the field opened to their research. The mysteries of the visible universe—the "wondrous works of Him which is perfect in knowledge" (Job 37:16)—invited man's study. Face-to-face, heart-to-heart communion with his Maker was his high privilege. Had he remained loyal to God, all this would have been his forever. Throughout eternal ages he would have continued to gain new treasures of knowledge, to discover fresh springs of happiness, and to obtain clearer and yet clearer conceptions of the wisdom, the power, and the love of God. More and more fully would he have fulfilled the object of his creation, more and more fully have reflected the Creator's glory.

But by disobedience this was forfeited. Through sin the divine likeness was marred, and well-nigh obliterated. Man's physical powers were weakened, his mental capacity was lessened, his spiritual vision dimmed. He had become subject to death. Yet the race was not left without hope. By infinite love and mercy the plan of salvation had been devised, and a life of probation was granted. To restore in man the image of his Maker, to bring him back to the perfection in which he was created, to promote the development of body, mind, and soul, that the divine purpose in his creation might be realized—this was to be the work of redemption. This is the object of education, the great object of life.

Love, the basis of creation and of redemption, is the basis of true education. This is made plain in the law that God has given as the guide of life. The first and great commandment is, "Thou shalt love the Lord thy God with all thy heart, and with all thy soul, and with all thy strength, and with all thy mind." Luke 10:27. To love Him, the infinite, the omniscient One, with the whole strength, and mind, and heart, means the highest development of every power. It means that in the whole being—the body, the mind, as well as the soul—the image of God is to be restored.

Like the first is the second commandment—"Thou shalt love thy neighbor as thyself." Matthew 22:39. The law of love calls for the devotion of body, mind, and soul to the service of God and our fellow men. And this service, while making us a blessing to others, brings the greatest blessing to ourselves. Unselfishness underlies all true development. Through unselfish service we receive the highest culture of every faculty. More and more fully do we become partakers of the divine nature. We are fitted for heaven, for we receive heaven into our hearts.

Since God is the source of all true knowledge, it is, as we have seen, the first object of education to direct our minds to His own revelation of Himself. Adam and Eve received knowledge through direct communion with God; and they learned of Him through His works. All created things, in their original perfection, were an expression of the thought of God. To Adam and Eve nature was teeming with divine wisdom. But by transgression man was cut off from learning of God through direct communion and, to a great degree, through His works. The earth, marred and defiled by sin, reflects but dimly the Creator's glory. It is true that His object lessons are not obliterated. Upon every page of the great volume of His created works may still be traced His handwriting. Nature still speaks of her Creator. Yet these revelations are partial and imperfect. And in our fallen state, with weakened powers and restricted vision, we are incapable of interpreting aright. We need the fuller revelation of Himself that God has given in His written word.

The Holy Scriptures are the perfect standard of truth, and as such should be given the highest place in education. To obtain an education worthy of the name, we must receive a knowledge of God, the Creator, and of Christ, the Redeemer, as they are revealed in the sacred word.

Every human being, created in the image of God, is endowed with a power akin to that of the Creator—individuality, power to think and to do. The men in whom this power is developed are the men who bear responsibilities, who are leaders in enterprise, and who influence character. It is the work of true education to develop this power, to train the youth to be thinkers, and not mere reflectors of other men's thought. Instead of confining their study to that which men have said or written, let students be directed to the sources of truth, to the vast fields opened for research in nature and revelation. Let them contemplate the great facts of duty and destiny, and the mind will expand and strengthen. Instead of educated weaklings, institutions of learning may send forth men strong to think and to act, men who are masters and not slaves of circumstances, men who possess breadth of mind, clearness of thought, and the courage of their convictions.

Such an education provides more than mental discipline; it provides more than physical training. It strengthens the character, so that truth and uprightness are not sacrificed to selfish desire or worldly ambition. It fortifies the mind against evil. Instead of some master passion becoming a power to destroy, every motive and desire are brought into conformity to the great principles of right. As the perfection of His character is dwelt upon, the mind is renewed, and the soul is re-created in the image of God.

What education can be higher than this? What can equal it in value?

> "It cannot be gotten for gold,
> Neither shall silver be weighed for the price thereof.
> It cannot be valued with the gold of Ophir,
> With the precious onyx, or the sapphire.
> The gold and the crystal cannot equal it
> And the exchange of it shall not be for jewels of fine gold.
> No mention shall be made of coral, or of pearls:
> For the price of wisdom is above rubies."
>
> Job 28:15-18.

Higher than the highest human thought can reach is God's ideal for His children. Godliness—godlikeness—is the goal to be reached. Before the student there is opened a path of continual progress. He has an object to achieve, a standard to attain, that includes everything good, and pure, and noble. He will advance as fast and as far as possible in every branch of true knowledge. But his efforts will be directed to objects as much higher than mere selfish and temporal interests as the heavens are higher than the earth.

He who co-operates with the divine purpose in imparting to the youth a knowledge of God, and molding the character into harmony with His, does a high and noble work. As he awakens a desire to reach God's ideal, he presents an education that is as high as heaven and as broad as the universe; an education that cannot be completed in this life, but that will be continued in the life to come; an education that secures to the successful student his passport from the preparatory school of earth to the higher grade, the school above.

2
The Eden School

"Happy is the man that findeth wisdom."

The system of education instituted at the beginning of the world was to be a model for man throughout all aftertime. As an illustration of its principles a model school was established in Eden, the home of our first parents. The Garden of Eden was the schoolroom, nature was the lesson book, the Creator Himself was the instructor, and the parents of the human family were the students.

Created to be "the image and glory of God" (1 Corinthians 11:7), Adam and Eve had received endowments not unworthy of their high destiny. Graceful and symmetrical in form, regular and beautiful in feature, their countenances glowing with the tint of health and the light of joy and hope, they bore in outward resemblance the likeness of their Maker. Nor was this likeness manifest in the physical nature only. Every faculty of mind and soul reflected the Creator's glory. Endowed with high mental and spiritual gifts, Adam and Eve were made but "little lower than the angels" (Hebrews 2:7), that they might not only discern the wonders of the visible universe, but comprehend moral responsibilities and obligations.

"The Lord God planted a garden eastward in Eden; and there He put the man whom He had formed. And out of the ground made the Lord God to grow every tree that is pleasant to the sight, and good for food; the tree of life also in the midst of the garden." Genesis 2:8,9. Here, amidst the beautiful scenes of nature untouched by sin, our first parents were to receive their education.

In His interest for His children, our heavenly Father personally directed their education. Often they were visited by His messengers, the holy angels, and from them received counsel and instruction. Often as they walked in the garden in the cool of the day they heard the voice of God, and face to face held communion with the Eternal. His thoughts toward them were "thoughts of peace, and not of evil." Jeremiah 29:11. His every purpose was their highest good.

To Adam and Eve was committed the care of the garden, "to dress it and to keep it." Genesis 2:15. Though rich in all that the Owner of the universe could supply, they were not to be idle. Useful occupation was appointed them as a blessing, to strengthen the body, to expand the mind, and to develop the character.

The book of nature, which spread its living lessons before them, afforded an exhaustless source of instruction and delight. On every leaf of the forest and stone of the mountains, in every shining star, in earth and sea and sky, God's name was written. With both the animate and the inanimate creation—with leaf and flower and tree, and with every living creature, from the leviathan of the waters to the mote in the sunbeam—the dwellers in Eden held converse, gathering from each the secrets of its life. God's glory in the heavens, the innumerable worlds in their orderly revolutions, "the balancings of the clouds" (Job 37:16), the mysteries of light and sound, of day and night—all were objects of study by the pupils of earth's first school.

The laws and operations of nature, and the great principles of truth that govern the spiritual universe, were opened to their minds by the infinite Author of all. In "the light of the knowledge of the glory of God" (2 Corinthians 4:6), their mental and spiritual powers developed, and they realized the highest pleasures of their holy existence.

As it came from the Creator's hand, not only the Garden of Eden but the whole earth was exceedingly beautiful. No taint of sin, or shadow of death, marred the fair creation. God's glory "covered the heavens, and the earth was full of His praise." "The morning stars sang together, and all the sons of God shouted for joy." Habakkuk 3:3; Job 38:7. Thus was the earth a fit emblem of Him who is "abundant in goodness and truth" (Exodus 34:6); a fit study for those who were made in His image. The Garden of Eden was a representation of what God desired the whole earth to become, and it was His purpose that, as the human family increased in numbers, they should establish other homes and schools like the one He had given. Thus in course of time the whole earth might be occupied with homes and schools where the words and the works of God should be studied, and where the students should thus be fitted more and more fully to reflect, throughout endless ages, the light of the knowledge of His glory.

3
The Knowledge of Good and Evil

"As they refused to have God in their knowledge," "their senseless heart was darkened."

Though created innocent and holy, our first parents were not placed beyond the possibility of wrong-doing. God might have created them without the power to transgress His requirements, but in that case there could have been no development of character; their service would not have been voluntary, but forced. Therefore He gave them the power of choice—the power to yield or to withhold obedience. And before they could receive in fullness the blessings He desired to impart, their love and loyalty must be tested.

In the Garden of Eden was the "tree of knowledge of good and evil. . . . And the Lord God commanded the man, saying, Of every tree of the garden thou mayest freely eat: but of the tree of the knowledge of good and evil, thou shalt not eat." Genesis 2:9-17. It was the will of God that Adam and Eve should not know evil. The knowledge of good had been freely given them; but the knowledge of evil—of sin and its results, of wearing toil, of anxious care, of disappointment and grief, of pain and death—this was in love withheld.

While God was seeking man's good, Satan was seeking his ruin. When Eve, disregarding the Lord's admonition concerning the forbidden tree, ventured to approach it, she came in contact with her foe. Her interest and curiosity having been awakened, Satan proceeded to deny God's word, and to insinuate distrust of His wisdom and goodness. To the woman's statement concerning the tree of knowledge, "God hath said, Ye shall not eat of it, neither shall ye touch it, lest ye die," the tempter made answer, "Ye shall not surely die: for God doth know that in the day ye eat thereof, then your eyes shall be opened, and ye shall be as gods, knowing good and evil." Genesis 3:3-5.

Satan desired to make it appear that this knowledge of good mingled with evil would be a blessing, and that in forbidding them to take of the fruit of the tree, God was withholding great good. He urged that it was because of its wonderful properties for imparting wisdom and power that God had forbidden them to taste it, that He was thus seeking to prevent them from reaching a nobler development and finding greater happiness. He declared that he himself had eaten of the forbidden fruit, and as a result had acquired the power of speech; and that if they also would eat of it, they would attain to a more exalted sphere of existence and enter a broader field of knowledge.

While Satan claimed to have received great good by eating of the forbidden tree, he did not let it appear that by transgression he had become an outcast from heaven. Here was falsehood, so concealed under a covering of apparent truth that Eve, infatuated, flattered, beguiled, did not discern the deception. She coveted what God had forbidden; she distrusted His wisdom. She cast away faith, the key of knowledge.

When Eve saw "that the tree was good for food, and that it was pleasant to the eyes, and a tree to be desired to make one wise, she took of the fruit thereof, and did eat." It was grateful to the taste, and, as she ate, she seemed to feel a vivifying power, and imagined herself entering upon a higher state of existence. Having herself transgressed, she became a tempter to her husband, "and he did eat." Genesis 3:6.

"Your eyes shall be opened," the enemy had said; "ye shall be as gods, knowing good and evil." Genesis 3:5. Their eyes were indeed opened; but how sad the opening! The knowledge of evil, the curse of sin, was all that the transgressors gained. There was nothing poisonous in the fruit itself, and the sin was not merely in yielding to appetite. It was distrust of God's goodness, disbelief of His word, and rejection of His authority, that made our first parents transgressors, and that brought into the world a knowledge of evil. It was this that opened the door to every species of falsehood and error.

Man lost all because he chose to listen to the deceiver rather than to Him who is Truth, who alone has understanding. By the mingling of evil with good, his mind had become confused, his mental and spiritual powers benumbed. No longer could he appreciate the good that God had so freely bestowed.

Adam and Eve had chosen the knowledge of evil, and if they ever regained the position they had lost they must regain it under the unfavorable conditions they had brought upon themselves. No longer were they to dwell in Eden, for in its perfection it could not teach them the lessons which it was now essential for them to learn. In unutterable sadness they bade farewell to their beautiful surroundings and went forth to dwell upon the earth, where rested the curse of sin.

To Adam God had said: "Because thou hast hearkened unto the voice of thy wife, and hast eaten of the tree, of which I commanded thee, saying, Thou shalt not eat of it: cursed is the ground for thy sake; in sorrow shalt thou eat of it all the days of thy life; thorns also and thistles shall it bring forth to thee; and thou shalt eat the herb of the field; in the sweat of thy face shalt thou eat bread, till thou return unto the ground; for out of it wast thou taken: for dust thou art, and unto dust shalt thou return." Genesis 3:17-19.

Although the earth was blighted with the curse, nature was still to be man's lesson book. It could not now represent goodness only; for evil was everywhere present, marring earth and sea and air with its defiling touch. Where once was written only the character of God, the knowledge of good, was now written also the character of Satan, the knowledge of evil. From nature, which now revealed the knowledge of good and evil, man was continually to receive warning as to the results of sin.

In drooping flower and falling leaf Adam and his companion witnessed the first signs of decay. Vividly was brought to their minds the stern fact that every living thing must die. Even the air, upon which their life depended, bore the seeds of death.

Continually they were reminded also of their lost dominion. Among the lower creatures Adam had stood as king, and so long as he remained loyal to God, all nature acknowledged his rule; but when he transgressed, this dominion was forfeited. The spirit of rebellion, to which he himself had given entrance, extended throughout the animal creation. Thus not only the life of man, but the nature of the beasts, the trees of the forest, the grass of the field, the very air he breathed, all told the sad lesson of the knowledge of evil.

But man was not abandoned to the results of the evil he had chosen. In the sentence pronounced upon Satan was given an intimation of redemption. "I will put enmity between thee and the woman," God said, "and between thy seed and her seed; it shall bruise thy head, and thou shalt bruise his heel." Genesis 3:15. This sentence, spoken in the hearing of our first parents, was to them a promise. Before they heard of the thorn and the thistle, of the toil and sorrow that must be their portion, or of the dust to which they must return, they listened to words that could not fail of giving them hope. All that had been lost by yielding to Satan could be regained through Christ.

This intimation also nature repeats to us. Though marred by sin, it speaks not only of creation but of redemption. Though the earth bears testimony to the curse in the evident signs of decay, it is still rich and beautiful in the tokens of life-giving power. The trees cast off their leaves, only to be robed with fresher verdure; the flowers die, to spring forth in new beauty; and in every manifestation of creative power is held out the assurance that we may be created anew in "righteousness and holiness of truth." Ephesians 4:24, margin. Thus the very objects and operations of nature that bring so vividly to mind our great loss become to us the messengers of hope.

As far as evil extends, the voice of our Father is heard, bidding His children see in its results the nature of sin, warning them to forsake the evil, and inviting them to receive the good.

4
Relation of Education to Redemption

"The light of the knowledge of the glory of God in the face of Jesus Christ."

By sin man was shut out from God. Except for the plan of redemption, eternal separation from God, the darkness of unending night, would have been his. Through the Saviour's sacrifice, communion with God is again made possible. We may not in person approach into His presence; in our sin we may not look upon His face; but we can behold Him and commune with Him in Jesus, the Saviour. "The light of the knowledge of the glory of God" is revealed "in the face of Jesus Christ." God is "in Christ, reconciling the world unto Himself." 2 Corinthians 4:6; 5:19.

"The Word became flesh, and dwelt among us, . . . full of grace and truth." "In Him was life; and the life was the light of men." John 1:14, R.V.; 1:4. The life and the death of Christ, the price of our redemption, are not only to us the promise and pledge of life, not only the means of opening again to us the treasures of wisdom: they are a broader, higher revelation of His character than even the holy ones of Eden knew.

And while Christ opens heaven to man, the life which He imparts opens the heart of man to heaven. Sin not only shuts us away from God, but destroys in the human soul both the desire and the capacity for knowing Him. All this work of evil it is Christ's mission to undo. The faculties of the soul, paralyzed by sin, the darkened mind, the perverted will, He has power to invigorate and to restore. He opens to us the riches of the universe, and by Him the power to discern and to appropriate these treasures is imparted.

Christ is the "Light, which lighteth every man that cometh into the world." John 1:9. As through Christ every human being has life, so also through Him every soul receives some ray of divine light. Not only intellectual but spiritual power, a perception of right, a desire for goodness, exists in every heart. But against these principles there is struggling an antagonistic power. The result of the eating of the tree of knowledge of good and evil is manifest in every man's experience. There is in his nature a bent to evil, a force which, unaided, he cannot resist. To withstand this force, to attain that ideal which in his inmost soul he accepts as alone worthy, he can find help in but one power. That power is Christ. Co-operation with that power is man's greatest need. In all educational effort should not this co-operation be the highest aim?

The true teacher is not satisfied with second-rate work. He is not satisfied with directing his students to a standard lower than the highest which it is possible for them to attain. He cannot be content with imparting to them only technical knowledge, with making them merely clever accountants, skillful artisans, successful tradesmen. It is his ambition to inspire them with principles of truth, obedience, honor, integrity, and purity—principles that will make them a positive force for the stability and uplifting of society. He desires them, above all else, to learn life's great lesson of unselfish service.

These principles become a living power to shape the character, through the acquaintance of the soul with Christ, through an acceptance of His wisdom as the guide, His power as the strength, of heart and life. This union formed, the student has found the Source of wisdom. He has within his reach the power to realize in himself his noblest ideals. The opportunities of the highest education for life in this world are his. And in the training here gained, he is entering upon that course which embraces eternity.

In the highest sense the work of education and the work of redemption are one, for in education, as in redemption, "other foundation can no man lay than that is laid, which is Jesus Christ." "It was the good pleasure of the Father that in Him should all the fullness dwell." 1 Corinthians 3:11; Colossians 1:19, R.V.

Under changed conditions, true education is still conformed to the Creator's plan, the plan of the Eden school. Adam and Eve received instruction through direct communion with God; we behold the light of the knowledge of His glory in the face of Christ.

The great principles of education are unchanged. "They stand fast for ever and ever" (Psalm 111:8); for they are the principles of the character of God. To aid the student in comprehending these principles, and in entering into that relation with Christ which will make them a controlling power in the life, should be the teacher's first effort and his constant aim. The teacher who accepts this aim is in truth a co-worker with Christ, a laborer together with God.

Illustrations

"Whatsoever things were written aforetime were written for our learning."

5
The Education of Israel

"The Lord alone did lead him;" "He instructed him, He kept him as the apple of His eye."

The system of education established in Eden centered in the family. Adam was "the son of God" (Luke 3:38), and it was from their Father that the children of the Highest received instruction. Theirs, in the truest sense, was a family school.

In the divine plan of education as adapted to man's condition after the Fall, Christ stands as the representative of the Father, the connecting link between God and man; He is the great teacher of mankind. And He ordained that men and women should be His representatives. The family was the school, and the parents were the teachers.

The education centering in the family was that which prevailed in the days of the patriarchs. For the schools thus established, God provided the conditions most favorable for the development of character. The people who were under His direction still pursued the plan of life that He had appointed in the beginning. Those who departed from God built for themselves cities, and, congregating in them, gloried in the splendor, the luxury, and the vice that make the cities of today the world's pride and its curse. But the men who held fast God's principles of life dwelt among the fields and hills. They were tillers of the soil and keepers of flocks and herds, and in this free, independent life, with its opportunities for labor and study and meditation, they learned of God and taught their children of His works and ways.

This was the method of education that God desired to establish in Israel. But when brought out of Egypt there were among the Israelites few prepared to be workers together with Him in the training of their children. The parents themselves needed instruction and discipline. Victims of lifelong slavery, they were ignorant, untrained, degraded. They had little knowledge of God and little faith in Him. They were confused by false teaching and corrupted by their long contact with heathenism. God desired to lift them to a higher moral level, and to this end He sought to give them a knowledge of Himself.

In His dealings with the wanderers in the desert, in all their marchings to and fro, in their exposure to hunger, thirst, and weariness, in their peril from heathen foes, and in the manifestation of His providence for their relief, God was seeking to strengthen their faith by revealing to them the power that was continually working for their good. And having taught them to trust in His love and power, it was His purpose to set before them, in the precepts of His law, the standard of character to which, through His grace, He desired them to attain.

Precious were the lessons taught to Israel during their sojourn at Sinai. This was a period of special training for the inheritance of Canaan. And their surroundings here were favorable for the accomplishing of God's purpose. On the summit of Sinai, overshadowing the plain where the people spread their tents, rested the pillar of cloud which had been the guide of their journey. A pillar of fire by night, it assured them of the divine protection; and while they were locked in slumber, the bread of heaven fell gently upon the encampment. On every hand, vast, rugged heights, in their solemn grandeur, spoke of eternal endurance and majesty. Man was made to feel his ignorance and weakness in the presence of Him who hath "weighed the mountains in scales, and the hills in a balance." Isaiah 40:12. Here, by the manifestation of His glory, God sought to impress Israel with the holiness of His character and requirements, and the exceeding guilt of transgression.

But the people were slow to learn the lesson. Accustomed as they had been in Egypt to material representations of the Deity, and these of the most degrading nature, it was difficult for them to conceive of the existence or the character of the Unseen One. In pity for their weakness, God gave them a symbol of His presence. "Let them make Me a sanctuary," He said; "that I may dwell among them." Exodus 25:8.

In the building of the sanctuary as a dwelling place for God, Moses was directed to make all things according to the pattern of things in the heavens. God called him into the mount, and revealed to him the heavenly things, and in their similitude the tabernacle, with all that pertained to it, was fashioned.

So to Israel, whom He desired to make His dwelling place, He revealed His glorious ideal of character. The pattern was shown them in the mount when the law was given from Sinai and when God passed by before Moses and proclaimed, "The Lord, The Lord God, merciful and gracious, long-suffering, and abundant in goodness and truth." Exodus 34:6.

But this ideal they were, in themselves, powerless to attain. The revelation at Sinai could only impress them with their need and helplessness. Another lesson the tabernacle, through its service of sacrifice, was to teach—the lesson of pardon of sin, and power through the Saviour for obedience unto life.

Through Christ was to be fulfilled the purpose of which the tabernacle was a symbol—that glorious building, its walls of glistening gold reflecting in rainbow hues the curtains inwrought with cherubim, the fragrance of ever-burning incense pervading all, the priests robed in spotless white, and in the deep mystery of the inner place, above the mercy seat, between the figures of the bowed, worshiping angels, the glory of the Holiest. In all, God desired His people to read His purpose for the human soul. It was the same purpose long afterward set forth by the apostle Paul, speaking by the Holy Spirit:

"Know ye not that ye are the temple of God, and that the Spirit of God dwelleth in you? If any man defile the temple of God, him shall God destroy; for the temple of God is holy, which temple ye are." 1 Corinthians 3:16, 17.

Great was the privilege and honor granted Israel in the preparation of the sanctuary; and great was also the responsibility. A structure of surpassing splendor, demanding for its construction the most costly material and the highest artistic skill, was to be erected in the wilderness, by a people just escaped from slavery. It seemed a stupendous task. But He who had given the plan of the building stood pledged to co-operate with the builders.

"The Lord spake unto Moses, saying, See, I have called by name Bezaleel the son of Uri, the son of Hur, of the tribe of Judah: and I have filled him with the Spirit of God, in wisdom, and in understanding, and in knowledge, and in all manner of workmanship. . . . And I, behold, I have given with him Aholiab, the son of Ahisamach, of the tribe of Dan: and in the hearts of all that are wisehearted I have put wisdom, that they may make all that I have commanded thee." Exodus 31:1-6.

What an industrial school was that in the wilderness, having for its instructors Christ and His angels!

In the preparation of the sanctuary and in its furnishing, all the people were to co-operate. There was labor for brain and hand. A great variety of material was required, and all were invited to contribute as their own hearts prompted.

Thus in labor and in giving they were taught to co-operate with God and with one another. And they were to co-operate also in the preparation of the spiritual building—God's temple in the soul.

From the outset of the journey from Egypt, lessons had been given for their training and discipline. Even before they left Egypt a temporary organization had been effected, and the people were arranged in companies, under appointed leaders. At Sinai the arrangements for organization were completed. The order so strikingly displayed in all the works of God was manifest in the Hebrew economy. God was the center of authority and government. Moses, as His representative, was to administer the laws in His name. Then came the council of seventy, then the priests and the princes, under these "captains over thousands, and captains over hundreds, and captains over fifties, and captains over tens" (Numbers 11:16, 17; Deuteronomy 1:15), and, lastly, officers appointed for special duties. The camp was arranged in exact order, the tabernacle, the abiding place of God, in the midst, and around it the tents of the priests and the Levites. Outside of these each tribe encamped beside its own standard.

Thoroughgoing sanitary regulations were enforced. These were enjoined on the people, not only as necessary to health, but as the condition of retaining among them the presence of the Holy One. By divine authority Moses declared to them, "The Lord thy God walketh in the midst of thy camp, to deliver thee; . . . therefore shall thy camp be holy." Deuteronomy 23:14.

The education of the Israelites included all their habits of life. Everything that concerned their well-being was the subject of divine solicitude, and came within the province of divine law. Even in providing their food, God sought their highest good. The manna with which He fed them in the wilderness was of a nature to promote physical, mental, and moral strength. Though so many of them rebelled against the restriction of their diet, and longed to return to the days when, they said, "We sat by the fleshpots, and when we did eat bread to the full" (Exodus 16:3), yet the wisdom of God's choice for them was vindicated in a manner they could not gainsay. Notwithstanding the hardships of their wilderness life, there was not a feeble one in all their tribes.

In all their journeyings the ark containing the law of God was to lead the way. The place of their encampment was indicated by the descent of the pillar of cloud. As long as the cloud rested over the tabernacle, they remained in camp. When it lifted, they pursued their journey. Both the halt and the departure were marked by a solemn invocation. "It came to pass, when the ark set forward, that Moses said, Rise up, Lord, and let Thine enemies be scattered. . . . And when it rested, he said, Return, O Lord, unto the many thousands of Israel." Numbers 10:35, 36.

As the people journeyed through the wilderness, many precious lessons were fixed in their minds by means of song. At their deliverance from Pharaoh's army the whole host of Israel had joined in the song of triumph. Far over desert and sea rang the joyous refrain, and the mountains re-echoed the accents of praise, "Sing ye to the Lord, for He hath triumphed gloriously." Exodus 15:21. Often on the journey was this song repeated, cheering the hearts and kindling the faith of the pilgrim travelers. The commandments as given from Sinai, with promises of God's favor and records of His wonderful works for their deliverance, were by divine direction expressed in song, and were chanted to the sound of instrumental music, the people keeping step as their voices united in praise.

Thus their thoughts were uplifted from the trials and difficulties of the way, the restless, turbulent spirit was soothed and calmed, the principles of truth were implanted in the memory, and faith was strengthened. Concert of action taught order and unity, and the people were brought into closer touch with God and with one another.

Of the dealing of God with Israel during the forty years of wilderness wandering, Moses declared: "As a man chasteneth his son, so the Lord thy God chasteneth thee;" "to humble thee, and to prove thee, to know what was in thine heart, whether thou wouldest keep His commandments, or no." Deuteronomy 8:5, 2.

"He found him in a desert land, and in the waste howling wilderness; He led him about, He instructed him, He kept him as the apple of His eye. As an eagle stirreth up her nest, fluttereth over her young, spreadeth abroad her wings, taketh them, beareth them on her wings: so the Lord alone did lead him, and there was no strange god with him." Deuteronomy 32:10-12.

"He remembered His holy promise, and Abraham His servant. And He brought forth His people with joy, and His chosen with gladness: and gave them the lands of the heathen: and they inherited the labor of the people; that they might observe His statutes, and keep His laws." Psalm 105:42-45.

God surrounded Israel with every facility, gave them every privilege, that would make them an honor to His name and a blessing to surrounding nations. If they would walk in the ways of obedience, He promised to make them "high above all nations which He hath made, in praise, and in name, and in honor." "All people of the earth," He said, "shall hear that thou art called by the name of the Lord; and they shall be afraid of thee." The nations which shall hear all these statutes shall say, "Surely this great nation is a wise and understanding people." Deuteronomy 26:19; 28:10; 4:6.

In the laws committed to Israel, explicit instruction was given concerning education. To Moses at Sinai God had revealed Himself as "merciful and gracious, long-suffering, and abundant in goodness and truth." Exodus 34:6. These principles, embodied in His law, the fathers and mothers in Israel were to teach their children. Moses by divine direction declared to them: "These words, which I command thee this day, shall be in thine heart: and thou shalt teach them diligently unto thy children, and shalt talk of them when thou sittest in thine house, and when thou walkest by the way, and when thou liest down, and when thou risest up." Deuteronomy 6:6, 7.

Not as a dry theory were these things to be taught. Those who would impart truth must themselves practice its principles. Only by reflecting the character of God in the uprightness, nobility, and unselfishness of their own lives can they impress others.

True education is not the forcing of instruction on an unready and unreceptive mind. The mental powers must be awakened, the interest aroused. For this, God's method of teaching provided. He who created the mind and ordained its laws, provided for its development in accordance with them. In the home and the sanctuary, through the things of nature and of art, in labor and in festivity, in sacred building and memorial stone, by methods and rites and symbols unnumbered, God gave to Israel lessons illustrating His principles and preserving the memory of His wonderful works. Then, as inquiry was made, the instruction given impressed mind and heart.

In the arrangements for the education of the chosen people it is made manifest that a life centered in God is a life of completeness. Every want He has implanted, He provides to satisfy; every faculty imparted, He seeks to develop.

The Author of all beauty, Himself a lover of the beautiful, God provided to gratify in His children the love of beauty. He made provision also for their social needs, for the kindly and helpful associations that do so much to cultivate sympathy and to brighten and sweeten life.

As a means of education an important place was filled by the feasts of Israel. In ordinary life the family was both a school and a church, the parents being the instructors in secular and in religious lines. But three times a year seasons were appointed for social intercourse and worship. First at Shiloh, and afterward at Jerusalem, these gatherings were held. Only the fathers and sons were required to be present; but none desired to forgo the opportunities of the feasts, and, so far as possible, all the household were in attendance; and with them, as sharers of their hospitality, were the stranger, the Levite, and the poor.

The journey to Jerusalem, in the simple, patriarchal style, amidst the beauty of the springtime, the richness of midsummer, or the ripened glory of autumn, was a delight. With offerings of gratitude they came, from the man of white hairs to the little child, to meet with God in His holy habitation. As they journeyed, the experiences of the past, the stories that both old and young still love so well, were recounted to the Hebrew children. The songs that had cheered the wilderness wandering were sung. God's commandments were chanted, and, bound up with the blessed influences of nature and of kindly human association, they were forever fixed in the memory of many a child and youth.

The ceremonies witnessed at Jerusalem in connection with the paschal service—the night assembly, the men with their girded loins, shoes on feet, and staff in hand, the hasty meal, the lamb, the unleavened bread, and the bitter herbs, and in the solemn silence the rehearsal of the story of the sprinkled blood, the death-dealing angel, and the grand march from the land of bondage—all were of a nature to stir the imagination and impress the heart.

The Feast of Tabernacles, or harvest festival, with its offerings from orchard and field, its week's encampment in the leafy booths, its social reunions, the sacred memorial service, and the generous hospitality to God's workers, the Levites of the sanctuary, and to His children, the strangers and the poor, uplifted all minds in gratitude to Him who had crowned the year with His goodness, and whose paths dropped fatness.

By the devout in Israel, fully a month of every year was occupied in this way. It was a period free from care and labor, and almost wholly devoted, in the truest sense, to purposes of education.

In apportioning the inheritance of His people, it was God's purpose to teach them, and through them the people of after generations, correct principles concerning the ownership of the land. The land of Canaan was divided among the whole people, the Levites only, as ministers of the sanctuary, being excepted. Though one might for a season dispose of his possession, he could not barter away the inheritance of his children. When able to do so, he was at liberty at any time to redeem it; debts were remitted every seventh year, and in the fiftieth, or year of jubilee, all landed property reverted to the original owner. Thus every family was secured in its possession, and a safeguard was afforded against the extremes either of wealth or of poverty.

By the distribution of the land among the people, God provided for them, as for the dwellers in Eden, the occupation most favorable to development—the care of plants and animals. A further provision for education was the suspension of agricultural labor every seventh year, the land lying fallow, and its spontaneous products being left to the poor. Thus was given opportunity for more extended study, for social intercourse and worship, and for the exercise of benevolence, so often crowded out by life's cares and labors.

Were the principles of God's laws regarding the distribution of property carried out in the world today, how different would be the condition of the people! An observance of these principles would prevent the terrible evils that in all ages have resulted from the oppression of the poor by the rich and the hatred of the rich by the poor. While it might hinder the amassing of great wealth, it would tend to prevent the ignorance and degradation of tens of thousands whose ill-paid servitude is required for the building up of these colossal fortunes. It would aid in bringing a peaceful solution of problems that now threaten to fill the world with anarchy and bloodshed.

The consecration to God of a tithe of all increase, whether of the orchard and harvest field, the flocks and herds, or the labor of brain or hand, the devotion of a second tithe for the relief of the poor and other benevolent uses, tended to keep fresh before the people the truth of God's ownership of all, and of their opportunity to be channels of His blessings. It was a training adapted to kill out all narrowing selfishness, and to cultivate breadth and nobility of character.

A knowledge of God, fellowship with Him in study and in labor, likeness to Him in character, were to be the source, the means, and the aim of Israel's education—the education imparted by God to the parents, and by them to be given to their children.

6
The Schools of the Prophets

"They sat down at Thy feet; everyone shall receive Thy words."

Wherever in Israel God's plan of education was carried into effect, its results testified of its Author. But in very many households the training appointed by Heaven, and the characters thus developed, were alike rare. God's plan was but partially and imperfectly fulfilled. By unbelief and by disregard of the Lord's directions, the Israelites surrounded themselves with temptations that few had power to resist. At their settlement in Canaan "they did not destroy the nations, concerning whom the Lord commanded them: but were mingled among the heathen, and learned their works. And they served their idols: which were a snare unto them." Their heart was not right with God, "neither were they steadfast in His covenant. But He, being full of compassion, forgave their iniquity, and destroyed them not: yea, many a time turned He His anger away. . . . For He remembered that they were but flesh; a wind that passeth away, and cometh not again." Psalms 106:34-36; 78:37-39. Fathers and mothers in Israel became indifferent to their obligation to God, indifferent to their obligation to their children. Through unfaithfulness in the home, and idolatrous influences without, many of the Hebrew youth received an education differing widely from that which God had planned for them. They learned the ways of the heathen.

To meet this growing evil, God provided other agencies as an aid to parents in the work of education. From the earliest times, prophets had been recognized as teachers divinely appointed. In the highest sense the prophet was one who spoke by direct inspiration, communicating to the people the messages he had received from God. But the name was given also to those who, though not so directly inspired, were divinely called to instruct the people in the works and ways of God. For the training of such a class of teachers, Samuel, by the Lord's direction, established the schools of the prophets.

These schools were intended to serve as a barrier against the widespreading corruption, to provide for the mental and spiritual welfare of the youth, and to promote the prosperity of the nation by furnishing it with men qualified to act in the fear of God as leaders and counselors. To this end, Samuel gathered companies of young men who were pious, intelligent, and studious. These were called the sons of the prophets. As they studied the word and the works of God, His life-giving power quickened the energies of mind and soul, and the students received wisdom from above. The instructors were not only versed in divine truth, but had themselves enjoyed communion with God, and had received the special endowment of His Spirit.

They had the respect and confidence of the people, both for learning and for piety. In Samuel's day there were two of these schools- one at Ramah, the home of the prophet, and the other at Kirjath-jearim. In later times others were established.

The pupils of these schools sustained themselves by their own labor in tilling the soil or in some mechanical employment. In Israel this was not thought strange or degrading; indeed, it was regarded as a sin to allow children to grow up in ignorance of useful labor. Every youth, whether his parents were rich or poor, was taught some trade. Even though he was to be educated for holy office, a knowledge of practical life was regarded as essential to the greatest usefulness. Many, also, of the teachers supported themselves by manual labor.

In both the school and the home much of the teaching was oral; but the youth also learned to read the Hebrew writings, and the parchment rolls of the Old Testament Scriptures were open to their study. The chief subjects of study in these schools were the law of God, with the instruction given to Moses, sacred history, sacred music, and poetry. In the records of sacred history were traced the footsteps of Jehovah. The great truths set forth by the types in the service of the sanctuary were brought to view, and faith grasped the central object of all that system—the Lamb of God, that was to take away the sin of the world. A spirit of devotion was cherished. Not only were the students taught the duty of prayer, but they were taught how to pray, how to approach their Creator, how to exercise faith in Him, and how to understand and obey the teachings of His Spirit. Sanctified intellect brought forth from the treasure house of God things new and old, and the Spirit of God was manifested in prophecy and sacred song.

These schools proved to be one of the means most effective in promoting that righteousness which "exalteth a nation." Proverbs 14:34. In no small degree they aided in laying the foundation of that marvelous prosperity which distinguished the reigns of David and Solomon.

The principles taught in the schools of the prophets were the same that molded David's character and shaped his life. The word of God was his instructor. "Through Thy precepts," he said, "I get understanding. . . . I have inclined mine heart to perform Thy statutes." Psalm 119:104-112. It was this that caused the Lord to pronounce David, when in his youth He called him to the throne, "a man after Mine own heart." Acts 13:22.

In the early life of Solomon also are seen the results of God's method of education. Solomon in his youth made David's choice his own. Above every earthly good he asked of God a wise and understanding heart. And the Lord gave him not only that which he sought, but that also for which he had not sought—both riches and honor. The power of his understanding, the extent of his knowledge, the glory of his reign, became the wonder of the world.

In the reigns of David and Solomon, Israel reached the height of her greatness. The promise given to Abraham and repeated through Moses was fulfilled: "If ye shall diligently keep all these commandments which I command you, to do them, to love the Lord your God, to walk in all His ways, and to cleave unto Him; then will the Lord drive out all these nations from before you, and ye shall possess greater nations and mightier than yourselves. Every place whereon the soles of your feet shall tread shall be yours: from the wilderness and Lebanon, from the river, the river Euphrates, even unto the uttermost sea shall your coast be. There shall no man be able to stand before you." Deuteronomy 11:22-25.

But in the midst of prosperity lurked danger. The sin of David's later years, though sincerely repented of and sorely punished, emboldened the people in transgression of God's commandments. And Solomon's life, after a morning of so great promise, was darkened with apostasy. Desire for political power and self-aggrandizement led to alliance with heathen nations. The silver of Tarshish and the gold of Ophir were procured by the sacrifice of integrity, the betrayal of sacred trusts. Association with idolaters, marriage with heathen wives, corrupted his faith. The barriers that God had erected for the safety of His people were thus broken down, and Solomon gave himself up to the worship of false gods. On the summit of the Mount of Olives, confronting the temple of Jehovah, were erected gigantic images and altars for the service of heathen deities. As he cast off his allegiance to God, Solomon lost the mastery of himself. His fine sensibilities became blunted. The conscientious, considerate spirit of his early reign was changed. Pride, ambition, prodigality, and indulgence bore fruit in cruelty and exaction. He who had been a just, compassionate, and God-fearing ruler, became tyrannical and oppressive. He who at the dedication of the temple had prayed for his people that their hearts might be undividedly given to the Lord, became their seducer. Solomon dishonored himself, dishonored Israel, and dishonored God.

The nation, of which he had been the pride, followed his leading. Though he afterward repented, his repentance did not prevent the fruition of the evil he had sown. The discipline and training that God appointed for Israel would cause them, in all their ways of life, to differ from the people of other nations. This peculiarity, which should have been regarded as a special privilege and blessing, was to them unwelcome. The simplicity and self-restraint essential to the highest development they sought to exchange for the pomp and self-indulgence of heathen peoples. To be "like all the nations" (1 Samuel 8:5) was their ambition. God's plan of education was set aside, His authority disowned.

In the rejection of the ways of God for the ways of men, the downfall of Israel began. Thus also it continued, until the Jewish people became a prey to the very nations whose practices they had chosen to follow.

As a nation the children of Israel failed of receiving the benefits that God desired to give them. They did not appreciate His purpose or co-operate in its execution. But though individuals and peoples may thus separate themselves from Him, His purpose for those who trust Him is unchanged. "Whatsoever God doeth, it shall be forever." Ecclesiastes 3:14.

While there are different degrees of development and different manifestations of His power to meet the wants of men in the different ages, God's work in all time is the same. The Teacher is the same. God's character and His plan are the same. With Him "is no variableness, neither shadow of turning." James 1:17.

The experiences of Israel were recorded for our instruction. "All these things happened unto them for ensamples: and they are written for our admonition, upon whom the ends of the world are come." 1 Corinthians 10:11. With us, as with Israel of old, success in education depends on fidelity in carrying out the Creator's plan. Adherence to the principles of God's word will bring as great blessings to us as it would have brought to the Hebrew people.

7
Lives of Great Men

"The fruit of the righteous is a tree of life."

Sacred history presents many illustrations of the results of true education. It presents many noble examples of men whose characters were formed under divine direction, men whose lives were a blessing to their fellow men and who stood in the world as representatives of God. Among these are Joseph and Daniel, Moses, Elisha, and Paul—the greatest statesmen, the wisest legislator, one of the most faithful of reformers, and, except Him who spoke as never man spake, the most illustrious teacher that this world has known.

In early life, just as they were passing from youth to manhood, Joseph and Daniel were separated from their homes and carried as captives to heathen lands. Especially was Joseph subject to the temptations that attend great changes of fortune. In his father's home a tenderly cherished child; in the house of Potiphar a slave, then a confidant and companion; a man of affairs, educated by study, observation, contact with men; in Pharaoh's dungeon a prisoner of state, condemned unjustly, without hope of vindication or prospect of release; called at a great crisis to the leadership of the nation—what enabled him to preserve his integrity?

No one can stand upon a lofty height without danger. As the tempest that leaves unharmed the flower of the valley uproots the tree upon the mountaintop, so do fierce temptations that leave untouched the lowly in life assail those who stand in the world's high places of success and honor. But Joseph bore alike the test of adversity and of prosperity. The same fidelity was manifest in the palace of the Pharaohs as in the prisoner's cell.

In his childhood, Joseph had been taught the love and fear of God. Often in his father's tent, under the Syrian stars, he had been told the story of the night vision at Bethel, of the ladder from heaven to earth, and the descending and ascending angels, and of Him who from the throne above revealed Himself to Jacob. He had been told the story of the conflict beside the Jabbok, when, renouncing cherished sins, Jacob stood conqueror, and received the title of a prince with God.

A shepherd boy, tending his father's flocks, Joseph's pure and simple life had favored the development of both physical and mental power. By communion with God through nature and the study of the great truths handed down as a sacred trust from father to son, he had gained strength of mind and firmness of principle.

In the crisis of his life, when making that terrible journey from his childhood home in Canaan to the bondage which awaited him in Egypt, looking for the last time on the hills that hid the tents of his kindred, Joseph remembered his father's God. He remembered the lessons of his childhood, and his soul thrilled with the resolve to prove himself true—ever to act as became a subject of the King of heaven.

In the bitter life of a stranger and a slave, amidst the sights and sounds of vice and the allurements of heathen worship, a worship surrounded with all the attractions of wealth and culture and the pomp of royalty, Joseph was steadfast. He had learned the lesson of obedience to duty. Faithfulness in every station, from the most lowly to the most exalted, trained every power for highest service.

At the time when he was called to the court of Pharaoh, Egypt was the greatest of nations. In civilization, art, learning, she was unequaled. Through a period of utmost difficulty and danger, Joseph administered the affairs of the kingdom; and this he did in a manner that won the confidence of the king and the people. Pharaoh "made him lord of his house, and ruler of all his substance: to bind his princes at his pleasure; and teach his senators wisdom." Psalm 105:21, 22.

The secret of Joseph's life Inspiration has set before us. In words of divine power and beauty, Jacob, in the blessing pronounced upon his children, spoke thus of his best-loved son:

> "Joseph is a fruitful bough,
> Even a fruitful bough by a well;
> Whose branches run over the wall:
> The archers have sorely grieved him,
> And shot at him, and hated him:
> But his bow abode in strength,
> And the arms of his hands were made strong
> By the hands of the mighty God of Jacob; . . .
> Even by the God of thy father, who shall help thee;
> And by the Almighty, who shall bless thee
> With blessings of heaven above,
> Blessings of the deep that lieth under: . . .
> The blessings of thy father have prevailed
> Above the blessings of my progenitors
> Unto the utmost bound of the everlasting hills:
> They shall be on the head of Joseph,
> And on the crown of the head of him that was separate
> from his brethren."
>
> Genesis 49:22-26.

Loyalty to God, faith in the Unseen, was Joseph's anchor. In this lay the hiding of his power.

> "The arms of his hands were made strong
> By the hands of the mighty God of Jacob."

Daniel, an Ambassador of Heaven

Daniel and his companions in Babylon were, in their youth, apparently more favored of fortune than was Joseph in the earlier years of his life in Egypt; yet they were subjected to tests of character scarcely less severe. From the comparative simplicity of their Judean home these youth of royal line were transported to the most magnificent of cities, to the court of its greatest monarch, and were singled out to be trained for the king's special service. Strong were the temptations surrounding them in that corrupt and luxurious court. The fact that they, the worshipers of Jehovah, were captives to Babylon; that the vessels of God's house had been placed in the temple of the gods of Babylon; that the king of Israel was himself a prisoner in the hands of the Babylonians, was boastfully cited by the victors as evidence that their religion and customs were superior to the religion and customs of the Hebrews. Under such circumstances, through the very humiliations that Israel's departure from His commandments had invited, God gave to Babylon evidence of His supremacy, of the holiness of His requirements, and of the sure result of obedience. And this testimony He gave, as alone it could be given, through those who still held fast their loyalty.

To Daniel and his companions, at the very outset of their career, there came a decisive test. The direction that their food should be supplied from the royal table was an expression both of the king's favor and of his solicitude for their welfare. But a portion having been offered to idols, the food from the king's table was consecrated to idolatry; and in partaking of the king's bounty these youth would be regarded as uniting in his homage to false gods. In such homage loyalty to Jehovah forbade them to participate. Nor dared they risk the enervating effect of luxury and dissipation on physical, mental, and spiritual development.

Daniel and his companions had been faithfully instructed in the principles of the word of God. They had learned to sacrifice the earthly to the spiritual, to seek the highest good. And they reaped the reward. Their habits of temperance and their sense of responsibility as representatives of God called to noblest development the powers of body, mind, and soul. At the end of their training, in their examination with other candidates for the honors of the kingdom, there was "found none like Daniel, Hananiah, Mishael, and Azariah." Daniel 1:19.

At the court of Babylon were gathered representatives from all lands, men of the choicest talents, men the most richly endowed with natural gifts, and possessed of the highest culture this world could bestow; yet amidst them all, the Hebrew captives were without a peer. In physical strength and beauty, in mental vigor and literary attainment, they stood unrivaled. "In all matters of wisdom and understanding, that the king inquired of them, he found them ten times better than all the magicians and astrologers that were in all his realm." Daniel 1:20.

Unwavering in allegiance to God, unyielding in the mastery of himself, Daniel's noble dignity and courteous deference won for him in his youth the "favor and tender love" of the heathen officer in whose charge he was. The same characteristics marked his life. Speedily he rose to the position of prime minister of the kingdom. Throughout the reign of successive monarchs, the downfall of the nation, and the establishment of a rival kingdom, such were his wisdom and statesmanship, so perfect his tact, his courtesy, and his genuine goodness of heart, combined with fidelity to principle, that even his enemies were forced to the confession that "they could find none occasion nor fault; forasmuch as he was faithful." Daniel 6:4.

While Daniel clung to God with unwavering trust, the spirit of prophetic power came upon him. While honored by men with the responsibilities of the court and the secrets of the kingdom, he was honored by God as His ambassador, and taught to read the mysteries of ages to come. Heathen monarchs, through association with Heaven's representative, were constrained to acknowledge the God of Daniel. "Of a truth it is," declared Nebuchadnezzar, "that your God is a God of gods, and a Lord of kings, and a revealer of secrets." And Darius, in his proclamation "unto all people, nations, and languages, that dwell in all the earth," exalted the "God of Daniel" as "the living God, and steadfast forever, and His kingdom that which shall not be destroyed;" who "delivereth and rescueth, and . . . worketh signs and wonders in heaven and in earth." Daniel 2:47; 6:25-27.

True and Honest Men

By their wisdom and justice, by the purity and benevolence of their daily life, by their devotion to the interests of the people—and they, idolaters—Joseph and Daniel proved themselves true to the principles of their early training, true to Him whose representatives they were. These men, both in Egypt and in Babylon, the whole nation honored; and in them a heathen people, and all the nations with which they were connected, beheld an illustration of the goodness and beneficence of God, an illustration of the love of Christ.

What a lifework was that of these noble Hebrews! As they bade farewell to their childhood home, how little did they dream of their high destiny! Faithful and steadfast, they yielded themselves to the divine guiding, so that through them God could fulfill His purpose.

The same mighty truths that were revealed through these men, God desires to reveal through the youth and the children of today. The history of Joseph and Daniel is an illustration of what He will do for those who yield themselves to Him and with the whole heart seek to accomplish His purpose.

The greatest want of the world is the want of men— men who will not be bought or sold, men who in their inmost souls are true and honest, men who do not fear to call sin by its right name, men whose conscience is as true to duty as the needle to the pole, men who will stand for the right though the heavens fall.

But such a character is not the result of accident; it is not due to special favors or endowments of Providence. A noble character is the result of self-discipline, of the subjection of the lower to the higher nature—the surrender of self for the service of love to God and man.

The youth need to be impressed with the truth that their endowments are not their own. Strength, time, intellect, are but lent treasures. They belong to God, and it should be the resolve of every youth to put them to the highest use. He is a branch, from which God expects fruit; a steward, whose capital must yield increase; a light, to illuminate the world's darkness.

Every youth, every child, has a work to do for the honor of God and the uplifting of humanity.

Elisha, Faithful in Little Things

The early years of the prophet Elisha were passed in the quietude of country life, under the teaching of God and nature and the discipline of useful work. In a time of almost universal apostasy his father's household were among the number who had not bowed the knee to Baal. Theirs was a home where God was honored and where faithfulness to duty was the rule of daily life.

The son of a wealthy farmer, Elisha had taken up the work that lay nearest. While possessing the capabilities of a leader among men, he received a training in life's common duties. In order to direct wisely, he must learn to obey. By faithfulness in little things, he was prepared for weightier trusts.

Of a meek and gentle spirit, Elisha possessed also energy and steadfastness. He cherished the love and fear of God, and in the humble round of daily toil he gained strength of purpose and nobleness of character, growing in divine grace and knowledge. While co-operating with his father in the home duties, he was learning to co-operate with God.

The prophetic call came to Elisha while with his father's servants he was plowing in the field. As Elijah, divinely directed in seeking a successor, cast his mantle upon the young man's shoulders, Elisha recognized and obeyed the summons. He "went after Elijah, and ministered unto him." 1 Kings 19:21. It was no great work that was at first required of Elisha; commonplace duties still constituted his discipline. He is spoken of as pouring water on the hands of Elijah, his master. As the prophet's personal attendant, he continued to prove faithful in little things, while with daily strengthening purpose he devoted himself to the mission appointed him by God.

When he was first summoned, his resolution had been tested. As he turned to follow Elijah he was bidden by the prophet to return home. He must count the cost—decide for himself to accept or reject the call. But Elisha understood the value of his opportunity. Not for any worldly advantage would he forgo the possibility of becoming God's messenger, or sacrifice the privilege of association with His servant.

As time passed, and Elijah was prepared for translation, so Elisha was prepared to become his successor. And again his faith and resolution were tested. Accompanying Elijah in his round of service, knowing the change soon to come, he was at each place invited by the prophet to turn back. "Tarry here, I pray thee," Elijah said; "for the Lord hath sent me to Bethel." But in his early labor of guiding the plow, Elisha had learned not to fail or to become discouraged; and now that he had set his hand to the plow in another line of duty, he would not be diverted from his purpose. As often as the invitation to turn back was given, his answer was, "As the Lord liveth, and as thy soul liveth, I will not leave thee." 2 Kings 2:2.

"And they two went on. . . . And they two stood by Jordan. And Elijah took his mantle, and wrapped it together, and smote the waters, and they were divided hither and thither, so that they two went over on dry ground. And it came to pass, when they were gone over, that Elijah said unto Elisha, Ask what I shall do for thee, before I be taken away from thee. And Elisha said, I pray thee, let a double portion of thy spirit be upon me. And he said, Thou hast asked a hard thing: nevertheless, if thou see me when I am taken from thee, it shall be so unto thee; but if not, it shall not be so. And it came to pass, as they still went on, and talked, that, behold, there appeared a chariot of fire, and horses of fire, and parted them both asunder; and Elijah went up by a whirlwind into heaven.

"And Elisha saw it, and he cried, My father, my father, the chariot of Israel, and the horsemen thereof. And he saw him no more: and he took hold of his own clothes, and rent them in two pieces. He took up also the mantle of Elijah that fell from him, and went back, and stood by the bank of Jordan; and he took the mantle of Elijah that fell from him, and smote the waters, and said, Where is the Lord God of Elijah? and when he also had smitten the waters, they parted hither and thither: and Elisha went over. And when the sons of the prophets which were to view at Jericho saw him, they said, The spirit of Elijah doth rest on Elisha. And they came to meet him, and bowed themselves to the ground before him." 2 Kings 2:6-15.

Henceforth Elisha stood in Elijah's place. And he who had been faithful in that which was least, proved himself faithful also in much.

Elijah, the man of power, had been God's instrument for the overthrow of gigantic evils. Idolatry, which, supported by Ahab and the heathen Jezebel, had seduced the nation, had been cast down. Baal's prophets had been slain.

The whole people of Israel had been deeply stirred, and many were returning to the worship of God. As successor to Elijah was needed one who by careful, patient instruction could guide Israel in safe paths. For this work Elisha's early training under God's direction had prepared him.

The lesson is for all. None can know what may be God's purpose in His discipline; but all may be certain that faithfulness in little things is the evidence of fitness for greater responsibilities. Every act of life is a revelation of character, and he only who in small duties proves himself "a workman that needeth not to be ashamed" (2 Timothy 2:15) will be honored by God with weightier trusts.

Moses, Powerful Through Faith

Younger than Joseph or Daniel was Moses when removed from the sheltering care of his childhood home; yet already the same agencies that shaped their lives had molded his. Only twelve years did he spend with his Hebrew kindred; but during these years was laid the foundation of his greatness; it was laid by the hand of one little known to fame.

Jochebed was a woman and a slave. Her lot in life was humble, her burden heavy. But through no other woman, save Mary of Nazareth, has the world received greater blessing. Knowing that her child must soon pass beyond her care, to the guardianship of those who knew not God, she the more earnestly endeavored to link his soul with heaven. She sought to implant in his heart love and loyalty to God. And faithfully was the work accomplished. Those principles of truth that were the burden of his mother's teaching and the lesson of her life, no after influence could induce Moses to renounce.

From the humble home in Goshen the son of Jochebed passed to the palace of the Pharaohs, to the Egyptian princess, by her to be welcomed as a loved and cherished son. In the schools of Egypt, Moses received the highest civil and military training. Of great personal attractions, noble in form and stature, of cultivated mind and princely bearing, and renowned as a military leader, he became the nation's pride. The king of Egypt was also a member of the priesthood; and Moses, though refusing to participate in the heathen worship, was initiated into all the mysteries of the Egyptian religion. Egypt at this time being still the most powerful and most highly civilized of nations, Moses, as its prospective sovereign, was heir to the highest honors this world could bestow. But his was a nobler choice. For the honor of God and the deliverance of His downtrodden people, Moses sacrificed the honors of Egypt. Then, in a special sense, God undertook his training.

Not yet was Moses prepared for his lifework. He had yet to learn the lesson of dependence upon divine power. He had mistaken God's purpose. It was his hope to deliver Israel by force of arms. For this he risked all, and failed. In defeat and disappointment he became a fugitive and exile in a strange land.

In the wilds of Midian, Moses spent forty years as a keeper of sheep. Apparently cut off forever from his life's mission, he was receiving the discipline essential for its fulfillment. Wisdom to govern an ignorant and undisciplined multitude must be gained through self-mastery. In the care of the sheep and the tender lambs he must obtain the experience that would make him a faithful, long-suffering shepherd to Israel. That he might become a representative of God, he must learn of Him.

The influences that had surrounded him in Egypt, the affection of his foster mother, his own position as the grandson of the king, the luxury and vice that allured in ten thousand forms, the refinement, the subtlety, and the mysticism of a false religion, had made an impression on his mind and character. In the stern simplicity of the wilderness all this disappeared.

Amidst the solemn majesty of the mountain solitudes Moses was alone with God. Everywhere the Creator's name was written. Moses seemed to stand in His presence and to be overshadowed by His power. Here his self-sufficiency was swept away. In the presence of the Infinite One he realized how weak, how inefficient, how short-sighted, is man.

Here Moses gained that which went with him throughout the years of his toilsome and care-burdened life—a sense of the personal presence of the Divine One. Not merely did he look down the ages for Christ to be made manifest in the flesh; he saw Christ accompanying the host of Israel in all their travels. When misunderstood and misrepresented, when called to bear reproach and insult, to face danger and death, he was able to endure "as seeing Him who is invisible." Hebrews 11:27.

Moses did not merely think of God, he saw Him. God was the constant vision before him. Never did he lose sight of His face.

To Moses faith was no guesswork; it was a reality. He believed that God ruled his life in particular; and in all its details he acknowledged Him. For strength to withstand every temptation, he trusted in Him.

The great work assigned him he desired to make in the highest degree successful, and he placed his whole dependence upon divine power. He felt his need of help, asked for it, by faith grasped it, and in the assurance of sustaining strength went forward.

Such was the experience that Moses gained by his forty years of training in the desert. To impart such an experience, Infinite Wisdom counted not the period too long or the price too great.

The results of that training, of the lessons there taught, are bound up, not only with the history of Israel, but with all which from that day to this has told for the world's progress. The highest testimony to the greatness of Moses, the judgment passed upon his life by Inspiration, is, "There arose not a prophet since in Israel like unto Moses, whom the Lord knew face to face." Deuteronomy 34:10.

Paul, Joyful in Service

With the faith and experience of the Galilean disciples who had companied with Jesus were united, in the work of the gospel, the fiery vigor and intellectual power of a rabbi of Jerusalem. A Roman citizen, born in a Gentile city; a Jew, not only by descent but by lifelong training, patriotic devotion, and religious faith; educated in Jerusalem by the most eminent of the rabbis, and instructed in all the laws and traditions of the fathers, Saul of Tarsus shared to the fullest extent the pride and the prejudices of his nation. While still a young man, he became an honored member of the Sanhedrin. He was looked upon as a man of promise, a zealous defender of the ancient faith.

In the theological schools of Judea the word of God had been set aside for human speculations; it was robbed of its power by the interpretations and traditions of the rabbis. Self-aggrandizement, love of domination, jealous exclusiveness, bigotry and contemptuous pride, were the ruling principles and motives of these teachers.

The rabbis gloried in their superiority, not only to the people of other nations, but to the masses of their own. With their fierce hatred of their Roman oppressors, they cherished the determination to recover by force of arms their national supremacy. The followers of Jesus, whose message of peace was so contrary to their schemes of ambition, they hated and put to death. In this persecution, Saul was one of the most bitter and relentless actors.

In the military schools of Egypt, Moses was taught the law of force, and so strong a hold did this teaching have upon his character that it required forty years of quiet and communion with God and nature to fit him for the leadership of Israel by the law of love. The same lesson Paul had to learn.

At the gate of Damascus the vision of the Crucified One changed the whole current of his life. The persecutor became a disciple, the teacher a learner. The days of darkness spent in solitude at Damascus were as years in his experience. The Old Testament Scriptures stored in his memory were his study, and Christ his teacher. To him also nature's solitudes became a school. To the desert of Arabia he went, there to study the Scriptures and to learn of God. He emptied his soul of prejudices and traditions that had shaped his life, and received instruction from the Source of truth.

His afterlife was inspired by the one principle of self-sacrifice, the ministry of love. "I am debtor," he said, "both to the Greeks, and to the barbarians; both to the wise, and to the unwise." "The love of Christ constraineth us." Romans 1:14; 2 Corinthians 5:14.

The greatest of human teachers, Paul accepted the lowliest as well as the highest duties. He recognized the necessity of labor for the hand as well as for the mind, and he wrought at a handicraft for his own support. His trade of tentmaking he pursued while daily preaching the gospel in the great centers of civilization. "These hands," he said, at parting with the elders of Ephesus, "have ministered unto my necessities, and to them that were with me." Acts 20:34.

While he possessed high intellectual endowments, the life of Paul revealed the power of a rarer wisdom. Principles of deepest import, principles concerning which the greatest minds of this time were ignorant, are unfolded in his teachings and exemplified in his life. He had that greatest of all wisdom, which gives quickness of insight and sympathy of heart, which brings man in touch with men, and enables him to arouse their better nature and inspire them to a higher life.

Listen to his words before the heathen Lystrians, as he points them to God revealed in nature, the Source of all good, who "gave us rain from heaven, and fruitful seasons, filling our hearts with food and gladness." Acts 14:17.

See him in the dungeon at Philippi, where, despite his pain-racked body, his song of praise breaks the silence of midnight. After the earthquake has opened the prison doors, his voice is again heard, in words of cheer to the heathen jailer, "Do thyself no harm: for we are all here" (Acts 16:28)—every man in his place, restrained by the presence of one fellow prisoner. And the jailer, convicted of the reality of that faith which sustains Paul, inquires the way of salvation, and with his whole household unites with the persecuted band of Christ's disciples.

See Paul at Athens before the council of the Areopagus, as he meets science with science, logic with logic, and philosophy with philosophy. Mark how, with the tact born of divine love, he points to Jehovah as "the Unknown God," whom his hearers have ignorantly worshiped; and in words quoted from a poet of their own he pictures Him as a Father whose children they are. Hear him, in that age of caste, when the rights of man as man were wholly unrecognized, as he sets forth the great truth of human brotherhood, declaring that God "hath made of one blood all nations of men for to dwell on all the face of the earth." Then he shows how, through all the dealings of God with man, runs like a thread of gold His purpose of grace and mercy. He "hath determined the times before appointed, and the bounds of their habitation; that they should seek the Lord, if haply they might feel after Him, and find Him, though He be not far from every one of us." Acts 17:23, 26, 27.

Hear him in the court of Festus, when King Agrippa, convicted of the truth of the gospel, exclaims, "Almost thou persuadest me to be a Christian." With what gentle courtesy does Paul, pointing to his own chain, make answer, "I would to God, that not only thou, but also all that hear me this day, were both almost, and altogether such as I am, except these bonds." Acts 26:28, 29.

Thus passed his life, as described in his own words, "in journeyings often, in perils of waters, in perils of robbers, in perils by mine own countrymen, in perils by the heathen, in perils in the city, in perils in the wilderness, in perils in the sea, in perils among false brethren; in weariness and painfulness, in watchings often, in hunger and thirst, in fastings often, in cold and nakedness." 2 Corinthians 11:26, 27.

"Being reviled," he said, "we bless; being persecuted, we suffer it: being defamed, we entreat; "as sorrowful, yet alway rejoicing; as poor, yet making many rich; as having nothing, and yet possessing all things." 1 Corinthians 4:12, 13; 2 Corinthians 6:10.

In service he found his joy; and at the close of his life of toil, looking back on its struggles and triumphs, he could say, "I have fought a good fight." 2 Timothy 4:7.

These histories are of vital interest. To none are they of deeper importance than to the youth. Moses renounced a prospective kingdom, Paul the advantages of wealth and honor among his people, for a life of burden bearing in God's service. To many the life of these men appears one of renunciation and sacrifice. Was it really so? Moses counted the reproach of Christ greater riches than the treasures in Egypt. He counted it so because it was so. Paul declared: "What things were gain to me, these have I counted loss for Christ. Yea verily, and I count all things to be loss for the excellency of the knowledge of Christ Jesus my Lord: for whom I suffered the loss of all things, and do count them but refuse, that I may gain Christ." Philippians 3:7, 8, R.V., margin. He was satisfied with his choice.

Moses was offered the palace of the Pharaohs and the monarch's throne; but the sinful pleasures that make men forget God were in those lordly courts, and he chose instead the "durable riches and righteousness." Proverbs 8:18. Instead of linking himself with the greatness of Egypt, he chose to bind up his life with God's purpose. Instead of giving laws to Egypt, he by divine direction enacted laws for the world. He became God's instrument in giving to men those principles that are the safeguard alike of the home and of society, that are the cornerstone of the prosperity of nations—principles recognized today by the world's greatest men as the foundation of all that is best in human governments.

The greatness of Egypt is in the dust. Its power and civilization have passed away. But the work of Moses can never perish. The great principles of righteousness which he lived to establish are eternal.

Moses' life of toil and heart-burdening care was irradiated with the presence of Him who is "the chiefest among ten thousand," and the One "altogether lovely." Song of Solomon 5:10, 16. With Christ in the wilderness wandering, with Christ on the mount of transfiguration, with Christ in the heavenly courts—his was a life on earth blessing and blessed, and in heaven honored.

Paul also in his manifold labors was upheld by the sustaining power of His presence. "I can do all things," he said, "through Christ which strengtheneth me." "Who shall separate us from the love of Christ? shall tribulation, or distress, or persecution, or famine, or nakedness, or peril, or sword? . . . Nay, in all these things we are more than conquerors through Him that loved us. For I am persuaded, that neither death, nor life, nor angels, nor principalities, nor powers, nor things present, nor things to come, nor height, nor depth, nor any other created thing (Rotherham's translation), shall be able to separate us from the love of God, which is in Christ Jesus our Lord." Philippians 4:13; Romans 8:35-39.

Yet there is a future joy to which Paul looked forward as the recompense of his labors—the same joy for the sake of which Christ endured the cross and despised the shame—the joy of seeing the fruition of his work. "What is our hope, or joy, or crown of rejoicing?" he wrote to the Thessalonian converts. "Are not even ye in the presence of our Lord Jesus Christ at His coming? For ye are our glory and joy." 1Thessalonians 2:19, 20.

Who can measure the results to the world of Paul's lifework? Of all those beneficent influences that alleviate suffering, that comfort sorrow, that restrain evil, that uplift life from the selfish and the sensual, and glorify it with the hope of immortality, how much is due to the labors of Paul and his fellow workers, as with the gospel of the Son of God they made their unnoticed journey from Asia to the shores of Europe?

What is it worth to any life to have been God's instrument in setting in motion such influences of blessing? What will it be worth in eternity to witness the results of such a lifework?

The Master Teacher

"Never man spake like this Man."

8
The Teacher Sent From God

"Consider Him."

"His name shall be called Wonderful, Counselor, The mighty God, The everlasting Father, The Prince of Peace." Isaiah 9:6.

In the Teacher sent from God, heaven gave to men its best and greatest. He who had stood in the councils of the Most High, who had dwelt in the innermost sanctuary of the Eternal, was the One chosen to reveal in person to humanity the knowledge of God.

Through Christ had been communicated every ray of divine light that had ever reached our fallen world. It was He who had spoken through everyone that throughout the ages had declared God's word to man. Of Him all the excellences manifest in the earth's greatest and noblest souls were reflections. The purity and beneficence of Joseph, the faith and meekness and long-suffering of Moses, the steadfastness of Elisha, the noble integrity and firmness of Daniel, the ardor and self-sacrifice of Paul, the mental and spiritual power manifest in all these men, and in all others who had ever dwelt on the earth, were but gleams from the shining of His glory. In Him was found the perfect ideal.

To reveal this ideal as the only true standard for attainment; to show what every human being might become; what, through the indwelling of humanity by divinity, all who received Him would become—for this, Christ came to the world. He came to show how men are to be trained as befits the sons of God; how on earth they are to practice the principles and to live the life of heaven.

God's greatest gift was bestowed to meet man's greatest need. The Light appeared when the world's darkness was deepest. Through false teaching the minds of men had long been turned away from God. In the prevailing systems of education, human philosophy had taken the place of divine revelation. Instead of the heaven-given standard of truth, men had accepted a standard of their own devising. From the Light of life they had turned aside to walk in the sparks of the fire which they had kindled.

Having separated from God, their only dependence being the power of humanity, their strength was but weakness. Even the standard set up by themselves they were incapable of reaching. The want of true excellence was supplied by appearance and profession. Semblance took the place of reality.

From time to time, teachers arose who pointed men to the Source of truth. Right principles were enunciated, and human lives witnessed to their power. But these efforts made no lasting impression. There was a brief check in the current of evil, but its downward course was not stayed. The reformers were as lights that shone in the darkness; but they could not dispel it. The world "loved darkness rather than light." John 3:19.

When Christ came to the earth, humanity seemed to be fast reaching its lowest point. The very foundations of society were undermined. Life had become false and artificial. The Jews, destitute of the power of God's word, gave to the world mind-benumbing, soul-deadening traditions and speculations. The worship of God "in Spirit and in truth" had been supplanted by the glorification of men in an endless round of man-made ceremonies. Throughout the world all systems of religion were losing their hold on mind and soul. Disgusted with fable and falsehood, seeking to drown thought, men turned to infidelity and materialism. Leaving eternity out of their reckoning, they lived for the present.

As they ceased to recognize the Divine, they ceased to regard the human. Truth, honor, integrity, confidence, compassion, were departing from the earth. Relentless greed and absorbing ambition gave birth to universal distrust. The idea of duty, of the obligation of strength to weakness, of human dignity and human rights, was cast aside as a dream or a fable. The common people were regarded as beasts of burden or as the tools and the stepping-stones for ambition. Wealth and power, ease and self-indulgence, were sought as the highest good. Physical degeneracy, mental stupor, spiritual death, characterized the age.

As the evil passions and purposes of men banished God from their thoughts, so forgetfulness of Him inclined them more strongly to evil. The heart in love with sin clothed Him with its own attributes, and this conception strengthened the power of sin. Bent on self-pleasing, men came to regard God as such a one as themselves—a Being whose aim was self-glory, whose requirements were suited to His own pleasure; a Being by whom men were lifted up or cast down according as they helped or hindered His selfish purpose. The lower classes regarded the Supreme Being as one scarcely differing from their oppressors, save by exceeding them in power. By these ideas every form of religion was molded. Each was a system of exaction. By gifts and ceremonies, the worshipers sought to propitiate the Deity in order to secure His favor for their own ends. Such religion, having no power upon the heart or the conscience, could be but a round of forms, of which men wearied, and from which, except for such gain as it might offer, they longed to be free. So evil, unrestrained, grew stronger, while the appreciation and desire for good diminished. Men lost the image of God and received the impress of the demoniacal power by which they were controlled. The whole world was becoming a sink of corruption.

There was but one hope for the human race—that into this mass of discordant and corrupting elements might be cast a new leaven; that there might be brought to mankind the power of a new life; that the knowledge of God might be restored to the world.

Christ came to restore this knowledge. He came to set aside the false teaching by which those who claimed to know God had misrepresented Him. He came to manifest the nature of His law, to reveal in His own character the beauty of holiness.

Christ came to the world with the accumulated love of eternity. Sweeping away the exactions which had encumbered the law of God, He showed that the law is a law of love, an expression of the Divine Goodness. He showed that in obedience to its principles is involved the happiness of mankind, and with it the stability, the very foundation and framework, of human society.

So far from making arbitrary requirements, God's law is given to men as a hedge, a shield. Whoever accepts its principles is preserved from evil. Fidelity to God involves fidelity to man. Thus the law guards the rights, the individuality, of every human being. It restrains the superior from oppression, and the subordinate from disobedience. It ensures man's well-being, both for this world and for the world to come. To the obedient it is the pledge of eternal life, for it expresses the principles that endure forever.

Christ came to demonstrate the value of the divine principles by revealing their power for the regeneration of humanity. He came to teach how these principles are to be developed and applied.

With the people of that age the value of all things was determined by outward show. As religion had declined in power, it had increased in pomp. The educators of the time sought to command respect by display and ostentation. To all this the life of Jesus presented a marked contrast. His life demonstrated the worthlessness of those things that men regarded as life's great essentials. Born amidst surroundings the rudest, sharing a peasant's home, a peasant's fare, a craftsman's occupation, living a life of obscurity, identifying Himself with the world's unknown toilers—amidst these conditions and surroundings—Jesus followed the divine plan of education. The schools of His time, with their magnifying of things small and their belittling of things great, He did not seek. His education was gained directly from the Heaven-appointed sources; from useful work, from the study of the Scriptures and of nature, and from the experiences of life—God's lesson books, full of instruction to all who bring to them the willing hand, the seeing eye, and the understanding heart.

"The Child grew, and waxed strong in spirit, filled with wisdom: and the grace of God was upon Him." Luke 2:40.

Thus prepared, He went forth to His mission, in every moment of His contact with men exerting upon them an influence to bless, a power to transform, such as the world had never witnessed.

He who seeks to transform humanity must himself understand humanity. Only through sympathy, faith, and love can men be reached and uplifted. Here Christ stands revealed as the master teacher; of all that ever dwelt on the earth, He alone has perfect understanding of the human soul.

"We have not a high priest"—master teacher, for the priests were teachers—"we have not a high priest that cannot be touched with the feeling of our infirmities; but One that hath been in all points tempted like as we are." Hebrews 4:15, R.V.

"In that He Himself hath suffered being tempted, He is able to succor them that are tempted." Hebrews 2:18.

Christ alone had experience in all the sorrows and temptations that befall human beings. Never another of woman born was so fiercely beset by temptation; never another bore so heavy a burden of the world's sin and pain. Never was there another whose sympathies were so broad or so tender. A sharer in all the experiences of humanity, He could feel not only for, but with, every burdened and tempted and struggling one.

What He taught, He lived. "I have given you an example," He said to His disciples; "that ye should do as I have done." "I have kept My Father's commandments." John 13:15; 15:10. Thus in His life, Christ's words had perfect illustration and support. And more than this; what He taught, He was. His words were the expression, not only of His own life experience, but of His own character. Not only did He teach the truth, but He was the truth. It was this that gave His teaching, power.

Christ was a faithful reprover. Never lived there another who so hated evil; never another whose denunciation of it was so fearless. To all things untrue and base His very presence was a rebuke. In the light of His purity, men saw themselves unclean, their life's aims mean and false. Yet He drew them. He who had created man, understood the value of humanity. Evil He denounced as the foe of those whom He was seeking to bless and to save. In every human being, however, fallen, He beheld a son of God, one who might be restored to the privilege of his divine relationship.

"God sent not His Son into the world to condemn the world; but that the world through Him might be saved." John 3:17. Looking upon men in their suffering and degradation, Christ perceived ground for hope where appeared only despair and ruin. Wherever there existed a sense of need, there He saw opportunity for uplifting. Souls tempted, defeated, feeling themselves lost, ready to perish, He met, not with denunciation, but with blessing.

The beatitudes were His greeting to the whole human family. Looking upon the vast throng gathered to listen to the Sermon on the Mount, He seemed for the moment to have forgotten that He was not in heaven, and He used the familiar salutation of the world of light. From His lips flowed blessings as the gushing forth of a long-sealed fountain.

Turning from the ambitious, self-satisfied favorites of this world, He declared that those were blessed who, however great their need, would receive His light and love. To the poor in spirit, the sorrowing, the persecuted, He stretched out His arms, saying, "Come unto Me, . . . and I will give you rest." Matthew 11:28.

In every human being He discerned infinite possibilities. He saw men as they might be, transfigured by His grace—in "the beauty of the Lord our God." Psalm 90:17. Looking upon them with hope, He inspired hope. Meeting them with confidence, He inspired trust. Revealing in Himself man's true ideal, He awakened, for its attainment, both desire and faith. In His presence souls despised and fallen realized that they still were men, and they longed to prove themselves worthy of His regard. In many a heart that seemed dead to all things holy, were awakened new impulses. To many a despairing one there opened the possibility of a new life.

Christ bound men to His heart by the ties of love and devotion; and by the same ties He bound them to their fellow men. With Him love was life, and life was service. "Freely ye have received," He said, "freely give." Matthew 10:8.

It was not on the cross only that Christ sacrificed Himself for humanity. As He "went about doing good" (Acts 10:38), every day's experience was an outpouring of His life. In one way only could such a life be sustained. Jesus lived in dependence upon God and communion with Him. To the secret place of the Most High, under the shadow of the Almighty, men now and then repair; they abide for a season, and the result is manifest in noble deeds; then their faith fails, the communion is interrupted, and the lifework marred. But the life of Jesus was a life of constant trust, sustained by continual communion; and His service for heaven and earth was without failure or faltering.

As a man He supplicated the throne of God, till His humanity was charged with a heavenly current that connected humanity with divinity. Receiving life from God, He imparted life to men.

"Never man spake like this Man." John 7:46. This would have been true of Christ had He taught only in the realm of the physical and the intellectual, or in matters of theory and speculation solely. He might have unlocked mysteries that have required centuries of toil and study to penetrate. He might have made suggestions in scientific lines that, till the close of time, would have afforded food for thought and stimulus for invention. But He did not do this. He said nothing to gratify curiosity or to stimulate selfish ambition. He did not deal in abstract theories, but in that which is essential to the development of character; that which will enlarge man's capacity for knowing God, and increase his power to do good. He spoke of those truths that relate to the conduct of life and that unite man with eternity.

Instead of directing the people to study men's theories about God, His word, or His works, He taught them to behold Him, as manifested in His works, in His word, and by His providences. He brought their minds in contact with the mind of the Infinite.

The people "were astonished at His teaching (R.V.), for His word was with power." Luke 4:32. Never before spoke one who had such power to awaken thought, to kindle aspiration, to arouse every capability of body, mind, and soul.

Christ's teaching, like His sympathies, embraced the world. Never can there be a circumstance of life, a crisis in human experience, which has not been anticipated in His teaching, and for which its principles have not a lesson. The Prince of teachers, His words will be found a guide to His co-workers till the end of time.

To Him the present and the future, the near and the far, were one. He had in view the needs of all mankind. Before His mind's eye was outspread every scene of human effort and achievement, of temptation and conflict, of perplexity and peril. All hearts, all homes, all pleasures and joys and aspirations, were known to Him.

He spoke not only for, but to, all mankind. To the little child, in the gladness of life's morning; to the eager, restless heart of youth; to men in the strength of their years, bearing the burden of responsibility and care; to the aged in their weakness and weariness—to all, His message was spoken—to every child of humanity, in every land and in every age.

In His teaching were embraced the things of time and the things of eternity—things seen, in their relation to things unseen, the passing incidents of common life and the solemn issues of the life to come.

The things of this life He placed in their true relation, as subordinate to those of eternal interest; but He did not ignore their importance. He taught that Heaven and earth are linked together, and that a knowledge of divine truth prepares man better to perform the duties of daily life.

To Him nothing was without purpose. The sports of the child, the toils of the man, life's pleasures and cares and pains, all were means to the one end—the revelation of God for the uplifting of humanity.

From His lips the word of God came home to men's hearts with new power and new meaning. His teaching caused the things of creation to stand out in new light. Upon the face of nature once more rested gleamings of that brightness which sin had banished. In all the facts and experiences of life were revealed a divine lesson and the possibility of divine companionship. Again God dwelt on earth; human hearts became conscious of His presence; the world was encompassed with His love. Heaven came down to men. In Christ their hearts acknowledged Him who had opened to them the science of eternity—

"Immanuel, . . . God with us."

In the Teacher sent from God, all true educational work finds its center. Of this work today as verily as of the work He established eighteen hundred years ago, the Saviour speaks in the words—

"I am the First and the Last, and the Living One."

"I am the Alpha and the Omega, the beginning and the end." Revelation 1:17, R.V.; 21:6, R.V.

In the presence of such a Teacher, of such opportunity for divine education, what worse than folly is it to seek an education apart from Him—to seek to be wise apart from Wisdom; to be true while rejecting Truth; to seek illumination apart from the Light, and existence without the Life; to turn from the Fountain of living waters, and hew out broken cisterns, that can hold no water.

Behold, He is still inviting: "If any man thirst, let him come unto Me, and drink. He that believeth on Me, as the Scripture hath said," out of him "shall flow rivers of living water." "The water that I shall give him shall become in him a well of water springing up unto eternal life." John 7:37, 38; 4:14, R.V.

9
An Illustration of His Methods

"I have manifested Thy name unto the men which Thou gavest Me."

The most complete illustration of Christ's methods as a teacher is found in His training of the twelve first disciples. Upon these men were to rest weighty responsibilities. He had chosen them as men whom He could imbue with His Spirit, and who could be fitted to carry forward His work on earth when He should leave it. To them, above all others, He gave the advantage of His own companionship. Through personal association He impressed Himself upon these chosen colaborers. "The Life was manifested," says John the beloved, "and we have seen it, and bear witness." 1 John 1:2.

Only by such communion—the communion of mind with mind and heart with heart, of the human with the divine—can be communicated that vitalizing energy which it is the work of true education to impart. It is only life that begets life.

In the training of His disciples the Saviour followed the system of education established at the beginning. The Twelve first chosen, with a few others who through ministry to their needs were from time to time connected with them, formed the family of Jesus. They were with Him in the house, at the table, in the closet, in the field. They accompanied Him on His journeys, shared His trials and hardships, and, as much as in them was, entered into His work.

Sometimes He taught them as they sat together on the mountainside, sometimes beside the sea, or from the fisherman's boat, sometimes as they walked by the way. Whenever He spoke to the multitude, the disciples formed the inner circle. They pressed close beside Him, that they might lose nothing of His instruction. They were attentive listeners, eager to understand the truths they were to teach in all lands and to all ages.

The first pupils of Jesus were chosen from the ranks of the common people. They were humble, unlettered men, these fishers of Galilee; men unschooled in the learning and customs of the rabbis, but trained by the stern discipline of toil and hardship. They were men of native ability and of teachable spirit; men who could be instructed and molded for the Saviour's work. In the common walks of life there is many a toiler patiently treading the round of his daily tasks, unconscious of latent powers that, roused to action, would place him among the world's great leaders. Such were the men who were called by the Saviour to be His colaborers. And they had the advantage of three years' training by the greatest educator this world has ever known.

In these first disciples was presented a marked diversity. They were to be the world's teachers, and they represented widely varied types of character. There were Levi Matthew the publican, called from a life of business activity, and subservience to Rome; the zealot Simon, the uncompromising foe of the imperial authority; the impulsive, self-sufficient, warmhearted Peter, with Andrew his brother; Judas the Judean, polished, capable, and mean-spirited; Philip and Thomas, faithful and earnest, yet slow of heart to believe; James the less and Jude, of less prominence among the brethren, but men of force, positive both in their faults and in their virtues; Nathanael, a child in sincerity and trust; and the ambitious, loving-hearted sons of Zebedee.

In order successfully to carry forward the work to which they had been called, these disciples, differing so widely in natural characteristics, in training, and in habits of life, needed to come into unity of feeling, thought, and action. This unity it was Christ's object to secure. To this end He sought to bring them into unity with Himself. The burden of His labor for them is expressed in His prayer to the Father, "that they all may be one; as Thou, Father, art in Me, and I in Thee, that they also may be one in Us: . . . that the world may know that Thou hast sent Me, and hast loved them, as Thou hast loved Me." John 17:21-23.

The Transforming Power of Christ

Of the twelve disciples, four were to act a leading part, each in a distinct line. In preparation for this, Christ taught them, foreseeing all. James, destined to swift-coming death by the sword; John, longest of the brethren to follow his Master in labor and persecution; Peter, the pioneer in breaking through the barriers of ages, and teaching the heathen world; and Judas, in service capable of pre-eminence above his brethren, yet brooding in his soul purposes of whose ripening he little dreamed—these were the objects of Christ's greatest solicitude and the recipients of His most frequent and careful instruction.

Peter, James, and John sought every opportunity of coming into close contact with their Master, and their desire was granted. Of all the Twelve their relationship to Him was closest. John could be satisfied only with a still near intimacy, and this he obtained. At that first conference beside the Jordan, when Andrew, having heard Jesus, hurried away to call his brother, John sat silent, rapt in the contemplation of wondrous themes. He followed the Saviour, ever an eager, absorbed listener. Yet John's was no faultless character. He was no gentle, dreamy enthusiast. He and his brother were called "the sons of thunder." Mark 3:17. John was proud, ambitious, combative; but beneath all this the divine Teacher discerned the ardent, sincere, loving heart. Jesus rebuked his self-seeking, disappointed his ambitions, tested his faith. But He revealed to him that for which his soul longed—the beauty of holiness, His own transforming love. "Unto the men which Thou gavest Me out of the world," He said to the Father, "I have manifested Thy name." John 17:6.

John's was a nature that longed for love, for sympathy and companionship. He pressed close to Jesus, sat by His side, leaned upon His breast. As a flower the sun and dew, so did he drink in the divine light and life. In adoration and love he beheld the Saviour, until likeness to Christ and fellowship with Him became his one desire, and in his character was reflected the character of his Master.

"Behold," he said, "what manner of love the Father hath bestowed upon us, that we should be called the sons of God: therefore the world knoweth us not, because it knew Him not. Beloved, now are we the sons of God, and it doth not yet appear what we shall be: but we know that, when He shall appear, we shall be like Him; for we shall see Him as He is. And every man that hath this hope in Him purifieth himself, even as He is pure." 1 John 3:1-3.

From Weakness to Strength

The history of no one of the disciples better illustrates Christ's method of training than does the history of Peter. Bold, aggressive, and self-confident, quick to perceive and forward to act, prompt in retaliation yet generous in forgiving, Peter often erred, and often received reproof. Nor were his warm-hearted loyalty and devotion to Christ the less decidedly recognized and commended. Patiently, with discriminating love, the Saviour dealt with His impetuous disciple, seeking to check his self-confidence, and to teach him humility, obedience, and trust.

But only in part was the lesson learned. Self-assurance was not uprooted.

Often Jesus, the burden heavy upon His own heart, sought to open to the disciples the scenes of His trial and suffering. But their eyes were holden. The knowledge was unwelcome, and they did not see. Self-pity, that shrank from fellowship with Christ in suffering, prompted Peter's remonstrance, "Pity Thyself, Lord: this shall not be unto Thee." Matthew 16:22, margin. His words expressed the thought and feeling of the Twelve.

So they went on, the crisis drawing nearer; they, boastful, contentious, in anticipation apportioning regal honors, and dreaming not of the cross.

For them all, Peter's experience had a lesson. To self-trust, trial is defeat. The sure outworking of evil still unforsaken, Christ could not prevent. But as His hand had been outstretched to save when the waves were about to sweep over Peter, so did His love reach out for his rescue when the deep waters swept over his soul. Over and over again, on the very verge of ruin, Peter's words of boasting brought him nearer and still nearer to the brink. Over and over again was given the warning, "Thou shalt . . . deny that thou knowest Me." Luke 22:34. It was the grieved, loving heart of the disciple that spoke out in the avowal, "Lord, I am ready to go with Thee, both into prison, and to death" (Luke 22:33); and He who reads the heart gave to Peter the message, little valued then, but that in the swift-falling darkness would shed a ray of hope: "Simon, Simon, behold, Satan hath desired to have you, that he may sift you as wheat: but I have prayed for thee, that thy faith fail not: and when thou art converted, strengthen thy brethren." Luke 22:31, 32.

When in the judgment hall the words of denial had been spoken; when Peter's love and loyalty, awakened under the Saviour's glance of pity and love and sorrow, had sent him forth to the garden where Christ had wept and prayed; when his tears of remorse dropped upon the sod that had been moistened with the blood drops of His agony—then the Saviour's words, "I have prayed for thee: . . . when thou art converted, strengthen thy brethren," were a stay to his soul. Christ, though foreseeing his sin, had not abandoned him to despair.

If the look that Jesus cast upon him had spoken condemnation instead of pity; if in foretelling the sin He had failed of speaking hope, how dense would have been the darkness that encompassed Peter! how reckless the despair of that tortured soul! In that hour of anguish and self-abhorrence, what could have held him back from the path trodden by Judas?

He who could not spare His disciple the anguish, left him not alone to its bitterness. His is a love that fails not nor forsakes.

Human beings, themselves given to evil, are prone to deal untenderly with the tempted and the erring. They cannot read the heart, they know not its struggle and pain. Of the rebuke that is love, of the blow that wounds to heal, of the warning that speaks hope, they have need to learn.

It was not John, the one who watched with Him in the judgment hall, who stood beside His cross, and who of the Twelve was first at the tomb—it was not John, but Peter, that was mentioned by Christ after His resurrection. "Tell His disciples and Peter," the angel said, "that He goeth before you into Galilee: there shall ye see Him." Mark 16:7.

At the last meeting of Christ with the disciples by the sea, Peter, tested by the thrice-given question, "Lovest thou Me?" was restored to his place among the Twelve. His work was appointed him; he was to feed the Lord's flock. Then, as His last personal direction, Jesus bade him, "Follow thou Me." John 21:17, 22.

Now he could appreciate the words. The lesson Christ had given when He set a little child in the midst of the disciples and bade them become like him, Peter could now better understand. Knowing more fully both his own weakness and Christ's power, he was ready to trust and to obey. In His strength he could follow his Master.

And at the close of his experience of labor and sacrifice, the disciple once so unready to discern the cross, counted it a joy to yield up his life for the gospel, feeling only that, for him who had denied the Lord, to die in the same manner as his Master died was too great an honor.

A miracle of divine tenderness was Peter's transformation. It is a life lesson to all seek to follow in the steps of the Master Teacher.

A Lesson in Love

Jesus reproved His disciples, He warned and cautioned them; but John and Peter and their brethren did not leave Him. Notwithstanding the reproofs, they chose to be with Jesus. And the Saviour did not, because of their errors, withdraw from them. He takes men as they are, with all their faults and weaknesses, and trains them for His service, if they will be disciplined and taught by Him.

But there was one of the Twelve to whom, until very near the close of His work, Christ spoke no word of direct reproof.

With Judas an element of antagonism was introduced among the disciples. In connecting himself with Jesus he had responded to the attraction of His character and life. He had sincerely desired a change in himself, and had hoped to experience this through a union with Jesus. But this desire did not become predominant. That which ruled him was the hope of selfish benefit in the worldly kingdom which he expected Christ to establish. Though recognizing the divine power of the love of Christ, Judas did not yield to its supremacy. He continued to cherish his own judgment and opinions, his disposition to criticize and condemn. Christ's motives and movements, often so far above his comprehension, excited doubt and disapproval, and his own questionings and ambitions were insinuated to the disciples. Many of their contentions for supremacy, much of their dissatisfaction with Christ's methods, originated with Judas.

Jesus, seeing that to antagonize was but to harden, refrained from direct conflict. The narrowing selfishness of Judas' life, Christ sought to heal through contact with His own self-sacrificing love. In His teaching He unfolded principles that struck at the root of the disciple's self-centered ambitions. Lesson after lesson was thus given, and many a time Judas realized that his character had been portrayed, and his sin pointed out; but he would not yield.

Mercy's pleading resisted, the impulse of evil bore final sway. Judas, angered at an implied rebuke and made desperate by the disappointment of his ambitious dreams, surrendered his soul to the demon of greed and determined upon the betrayal of his Master. From the Passover chamber, the joy of Christ's presence, and the light of immortal hope, he went forth to his evil work—into the outer darkness, where hope was not.

"Jesus knew from the beginning who they were that believed not, and who should betray Him." John 6:64. Yet, knowing all, He had withheld no pleading of mercy or gift of love.

Seeing the danger of Judas, He had brought him close to Himself, within the inner circle of His chosen and trusted disciples. Day after day, when the burden lay heaviest upon His own heart, He had borne the pain of continual contact with that stubborn, suspicious, brooding spirit; He had witnessed and labored to counteract among His disciples that continuous, secret, and subtle antagonism. And all this that no possible saving influence might be lacking to that imperiled soul!

> "Many waters cannot quench love,
> Neither can the floods drown it;"
> "For love is strong as death."
>
> Song of Solomon 8:7, 6.

So far as Judas himself was concerned, Christ's work of love had been without avail. But not so as regards his fellow disciples. To them it was a lesson of lifelong influence. Ever would its example of tenderness and long-suffering mold their intercourse with the tempted and the erring. And it had other lessons. At the ordination of the Twelve the disciples had greatly desired that Judas should become one of their number, and they had counted his accession an event of much promise to the apostolic band. He had come more into contact with the world than they, he was a man of good address, of discernment and executive ability, and, having a high estimate of his own qualifications, he had led the disciples to hold him in the same regard. But the methods he desired to introduce into Christ's work were based upon worldly principles and were controlled by worldly policy. They looked to the securing of worldly recognition and honor—to the obtaining of the kingdom of this world. The working out of these desires in the life of Judas, helped the disciples to understand the antagonism between the principle of self-aggrandizement and Christ's principle of humility and self-sacrifice—the principle of the spiritual kingdom. In the fate of Judas they saw the end to which self-serving tends.

For these disciples the mission of Christ finally accomplished its purpose. Little by little His example and His lessons of self-abnegation molded their characters. His death destroyed their hope of worldly greatness. The fall of Peter, the apostasy of Judas, their own failure in forsaking Christ in His anguish and peril, swept away their self-sufficiency. They saw their own weakness; they saw something of the greatness of the work committed to them; they felt their need of their Master's guidance at every step.

They knew that His personal presence was no longer to be with them, and they recognized, as they had never recognized before, the value of the opportunities that had been theirs to walk and talk with the Sent of God. Many of His lessons, when spoken, they had not appreciated or understood; now they longed to recall these lessons, to hear again His words. With what joy now came back to them His assurance:

"It is expedient for you that I go away; for if I go not away, the Comforter will not come unto you; but if I depart, I will send Him." "All things that I have heard of My Father I have made known unto you." And "the Comforter, . . . whom the Father will send in My name, He shall teach you all things, and bring all things to your remembrance, whatsoever I have said unto you." John 16:7; 15:15; 14:26.

"All things that the Father hath are Mine." "When He, the Spirit of truth, is come, He will guide you into all truth. . . . He shall receive of Mine, and shall show it unto you." John 16:15, 13, 14.

The disciples had seen Christ ascend from among them on the Mount of Olives. And as the heavens received Him, there had come back to them His parting promise, "Lo, I am with you alway, even unto the end of the world." Matthew 28:20.

They knew that His sympathies were with them still. They knew that they had a representative, an advocate, at the throne of God. In the name of Jesus they presented their petitions, repeating His promise, "Whatsoever ye shall ask the Father in My name, He will give it you." John 16:23.

Higher and higher they extended the hand of faith, with the mighty argument, "It is Christ that died, yea rather, that is risen again, who is even at the right hand of God, who also maketh intercession for us." Romans 8:34.

Faithful to his promise, the Divine One, exalted in the heavenly courts, imparted of His fullness to His followers on earth. His enthronement at God's right hand was signalized by the outpouring of the Spirit upon His disciples.

By the work of Christ these disciples had been led to feel their need of the Spirit; under the Spirit's teaching they received their final preparation and went forth to their lifework.

No longer were they ignorant and uncultured. No longer were they a collection of independent units or of discordant and conflicting elements. No longer were their hopes set on worldly greatness. They were of "one accord," of one mind and one soul. Christ filled their thoughts. The advancement of His kingdom was their aim. In mind and character they had become like their Master; and men "took knowledge of them, that they had been with Jesus." Acts 4:13.

Then was there such a revelation of the glory of Christ as had never before been witnessed by mortal man. Multitudes who had reviled His name and despised His power confessed themselves disciples of the Crucified. Through the co-operation of the divine Spirit the labors of the humble men whom Christ had chosen stirred the world. To every nation under heaven was the gospel carried in a single generation.

The same Spirit that in His stead was sent to be the instructor of His first co-workers, Christ has commissioned to be the instructor of His co-workers today. "Lo, I am with you alway, even unto the end of the world" (Matthew 28:20), is His promise.

The presence of the same guide in educational work today will produce the same results as of old. This is the end to which true education tends; this is the work that God designs it to accomplish.

Nature Teaching

"Consider . . . the wondrous works of Him which is perfect in knowledge."

10
God in Nature

"His glory covered the heavens, and the earth was full of His praise."

Upon all created things is seen the impress of the Deity. Nature testifies of God. The susceptible mind, brought in contact with the miracle and mystery of the universe, cannot but recognize the working of infinite power. Not by its own inherent energy does the earth produce its bounties, and year by year continue its motion around the sun. An unseen hand guides the planets in their circuit of the heavens. A mysterious life pervades all nature—a life that sustains the unnumbered worlds throughout immensity, that lives in the insect atom which floats in the summer breeze, that wings the flight of the swallow and feeds the young ravens which cry, that brings the bud to blossom and the flower to fruit.

The same power that upholds nature, is working also in man. The same great laws that guide alike the star and the atom control human life. The laws that govern the heart's action, regulating the flow of the current of life to the body, are the laws of the mighty Intelligence that has the jurisdiction of the soul. From Him all life proceeds. Only in harmony with Him can be found its true sphere of action. For all the objects of His creation the condition is the same—a life sustained by receiving the life of God, a life exercised in harmony with the Creator's will. To transgress His law, physical, mental, or moral, is to place one's self out of harmony with the universe, to introduce discord, anarchy, ruin.

To him who learns thus to interpret its teachings, all nature becomes illuminated; the world is a lesson book, life a school. The unity of man with nature and with God, the universal dominion of law, the results of transgression, cannot fail of impressing the mind and molding the character.

These are lessons that our children need to learn. To the little child, not yet capable of learning from the printed page or of being introduced to the routine of the schoolroom, nature presents an unfailing source of instruction and delight. The heart not yet hardened by contact with evil is quick to recognize the Presence that pervades all created things. The ear as yet undulled by the world's clamor is attentive to the Voice that speaks through nature's utterances. And for those of older years, needing continually its silent reminders of the spiritual and eternal, nature's teaching will be no less a source of pleasure and of instruction. As the dwellers in Eden learned from nature's pages, as Moses discerned God's handwriting on the Arabian plains and mountains, and the child Jesus on the hillsides of Nazareth, so the children of today may learn of Him. The unseen is illustrated by the seen. On everything upon the earth, from the loftiest tree of the forest to the lichen that clings to the rock, from the boundless ocean to the tiniest shell on the shore, they may behold the image and superscription of God.

So far as possible, let the child from his earliest years be placed where this wonderful lesson book shall be open before him. Let him behold the glorious scenes painted by the great Master Artist upon the shifting canvas of the heavens, let him become acquainted with the wonders of earth and sea, let him watch the unfolding mysteries of the changing seasons, and, in all His works, learn of the Creator.

In no other way can the foundation of a true education be so firmly and surely laid. Yet even the child, as he comes in contact with nature, will see cause for perplexity. He cannot but recognize the working of antagonistic forces. It is here that nature needs an interpreter. Looking upon the evil manifest even in the natural world, all have the same sorrowful lesson to learn—"An enemy hath done this." Matthew 13:28.

Only in the light that shines from Calvary can nature's teaching be read aright. Through the story of Bethlehem and the cross let it be shown how good is to conquer evil, and how every blessing that comes to us is a gift of redemption.

In brier and thorn, in thistle and tare, is represented the evil that blights and mars. In singing bird and opening blossom, in rain and sunshine, in summer breeze and gentle dew, in ten thousand objects in nature, from the oak of the forest to the violet that blossoms at its root, is seen the love that restores. And nature still speaks to us of God's goodness.

"I know the thoughts that I think toward you, saith the Lord, thoughts of peace, and not of evil." Jeremiah 29:11. This is the message that, in the light from the cross, may be read upon all the face of nature. The heavens declare His glory, and the earth is full of His riches.

11
Lessons of Life

"Speak to the earth, and it shall teach thee."

The Great Teacher brought His hearers in contact with nature, that they might listen to the voice which speaks in all created things; and as their hearts became tender and their minds receptive, He helped them to interpret the spiritual teaching of the scenes upon which their eyes rested. The parables, by means of which He loved to teach lessons of truth, show how open His spirit was to the influences of nature and how He delighted to gather the spiritual teaching from the surroundings of daily life.

The birds of the air, the lilies of the field, the sower and the seed, the shepherd and the sheep—with these Christ illustrated immortal truth. He drew illustrations also from the events of life, facts of experience familiar to the hearers—the leaven, the hid treasure, the pearl, the fishing net, the lost coin, the prodigal son, the houses on the rock and the sand. In His lessons there was something to interest every mind, to appeal to every heart. Thus the daily task, instead of being a mere round of toil, bereft of higher thoughts, was brightened and uplifted by constant reminders of the spiritual and the unseen.

So we should teach. Let the children learn to see in nature an expression of the love and the wisdom of God; let the thought of Him be linked with bird and flower and tree; let all things seen become to them the interpreters of the unseen, and all the events of life be a means of divine teaching.

As they learn thus to study the lessons in all created things, and in all life's experiences, show that the same laws which govern the things of nature and the events of life are to control us; that they are given for our good; and that only in obedience to them can we find true happiness and success.

The Law of Ministry

All things both in heaven and in earth declare that the great law of life is a law of service. The infinite Father ministers to the life of every living thing. Christ came to the earth "as He that serveth." Luke 22:27. The angels are "ministering spirits, sent forth to minister for them who shall be heirs of salvation." Hebrews 1:14. The same law of service is written upon all things in nature. The birds of the air, the beasts of the field, the trees of the forest, the leaves, the grass, and the flowers, the sun in the heavens and the stars of light—all have their ministry. Lake and ocean, river and water spring—each takes to give.

As each thing in nature ministers thus to the world's life, it also secures its own. "Give, and it shall be given unto you" (Luke 6:38), is the lesson written no less surely in nature than in the pages of Holy Writ.

As the hillsides and the plains open a channel for the mountain stream to reach the sea, that which they give is repaid a hundredfold. The stream that goes singing on its way leaves behind its gift of beauty and fruitfulness. Through the fields, bare and brown under the summer's heat, a line of verdure marks the river's course; every noble tree, every bud, every blossom, a witness to the recompense God's grace decrees to all who become its channels to the world.

Sowing in Faith

Of the almost innumerable lessons taught in the varied processes of growth, some of the most precious are conveyed in the Saviour's parable of the growing seed. It has lessons for old and young.

"So is the kingdom of God, as if a man should cast seed into the ground; and should sleep, and rise night and day, and the seed should spring and grow up, he knoweth not how. For the earth bringeth forth fruit of herself; first the blade, then the ear, after that the full corn in the ear." Mark 4:26-28.

The seed has in itself a germinating principle, a principle that God Himself has implanted; yet if left to itself the seed would have no power to spring up. Man has his part to act in promoting the growth of the grain; but there is a point beyond which he can accomplish nothing. He must depend upon One who has connected the sowing and the reaping by wonderful links of His own omnipotent power.

There is life in the seed, there is power in the soil; but unless infinite power is exercised day and night, the seed will yield no return. The showers of rain must refresh the thirsty fields; the sun must impart warmth; electricity must be conveyed to the buried seed. The life which the Creator has implanted, He alone can call forth. Every seed grows, every plant develops, by the power of God.

"The seed is the word of God." "As the earth bringeth forth her bud, and as the garden causeth the things that are sown in it to spring forth; so the Lord God will cause righteousness and praise to spring forth." Luke 8:11; Isaiah 61:11. As in the natural, so in the spiritual sowing; the power that alone can produce life is from God.

The work of the sower is a work of faith. The mystery of the germination and growth of the seed he cannot understand; but he has confidence in the agencies by which God causes vegetation to flourish. He casts away the seed, expecting to gather it manyfold in an abundant harvest. So parents and teachers are to labor, expecting a harvest from the seed they sow.

For a time the good seed may lie unnoticed in the heart, giving no evidence that it has taken root; but afterward, as the Spirit of God breathes on the soul, the hidden seed springs up, and at last brings forth fruit. In our lifework we know not which shall prosper, this or that. This question it is not for us to settle. "In the morning sow thy seed, and in the evening withhold not thine hand." Ecclesiastes 11:6. God's great covenant declares that "while the earth remaineth, seedtime and harvest . . . shall not cease." Genesis 8:22. In the confidence of this promise the husbandman tills and sows. Not less confidently are we, in the spiritual sowing, to labor, trusting His assurance: "So shall My word be that goeth forth out of My mouth: it shall not return unto Me void, but it shall accomplish that which I please, and it shall prosper in the thing whereto I sent it." "He that goeth forth and weepeth, bearing precious seed, shall doubtless come again with rejoicing, bringing his sheaves with him." Isaiah 55:11; Psalm 126:6.

The germination of the seed represents the beginning of spiritual life, and the development of the plant is a figure of the development of character. There can be no life without growth. The plant must either grow or die. As its growth is silent and imperceptible, but continuous, so is the growth of character. At every stage of development our life may be perfect; yet if God's purpose for us is fulfilled, there will be constant advancement.

The plant grows by receiving that which God has provided to sustain its life. So spiritual growth is attained through co-operation with divine agencies. As the plant takes root in the soil, so we are to take root in Christ. As the plant receives the sunshine, the dew, and the rain, so are we to receive the Holy Spirit. If our hearts are stayed upon Christ, He will come unto us "as the rain, as the latter and former rain unto the earth." As the Sun of Righteousness, He will arise upon us "with healing in His wings." We shall "grow as the lily." We "shall revive as the corn, and grow as the vine." Hosea 6:3; Malachi 4:2; Hosea 14:5, 7.

The wheat develops, "first the blade, then the ear, after that the full corn in the ear." Mark 4:28. The object of the husbandman in the sowing of the seed and the culture of the plant, is the production of grain—bread for the hungry, and seed for future harvests. So the divine Husbandman looks for a harvest. He is seeking to reproduce Himself in the hearts and lives of His followers, that through them He may be reproduced in other hearts and lives.

The gradual development of the plant from the seed is an object lesson in child training. There is "first the blade, then the ear, after that the full corn in the ear." Mark 4:28. He who gave this parable created the tiny seed, gave it its vital properties, and ordained the laws that govern its growth. And the truths taught by the parable were made a reality in His own life. He, the Majesty of heaven, the King of glory, became a babe in Bethlehem, and for a time represented the helpless infant in its mother's care. In childhood He spoke and acted as a child, honoring His parents, and carrying out their wishes in helpful ways. But from the first dawning of intelligence He was constantly growing in grace and in a knowledge of truth.

Parents and teachers should aim so to cultivate the tendencies of the youth that at each stage of life they may represent the beauty appropriate to that period, unfolding naturally, as do the plants in the garden.

The little ones should be educated in childlike simplicity. They should be trained to be content with the small, helpful duties and the pleasures and experiences natural to their years. Childhood answers to the blade in the parable, and the blade has a beauty peculiarly its own. Children should not be forced into a precocious maturity, but as long as possible should retain the freshness and grace of their early years. The more quiet and simple the life of the child—the more free from artificial excitement and the more in harmony with nature—the more favorable it is to physical and mental vigor and to spiritual strength.

In the Saviour's miracle of feeding the five thousand is illustrated the working of God's power in the production of the harvest. Jesus draws aside the veil from the world of nature and reveals the creative energy that is constantly exercised for our good. In multiplying the seed cast into the ground, He who multiplied the loaves is working a miracle every day. It is by miracle that He constantly feeds millions from earth's harvest fields. Men are called upon to co-operate with Him in the care of the grain and the preparation of the loaf, and because of this they lose sight of the divine agency. The working of His power is ascribed to natural causes or to human instrumentality, and too often His gifts are perverted to selfish uses and made a curse instead of a blessing. God is seeking to change all this. He desires that our dull senses shall be quickened to discern His merciful kindness, that His gifts may be to us the blessing that He intended.

It is the word of God, the impartation of His life, that gives life to the seed; and of that life, we, in eating the grain, become partakers. This, God desires us to discern; He desires that even in receiving our daily bread we may recognize His agency and may be brought into closer fellowship with Him.

By the laws of God in nature, effect follows cause with unvarying certainty. The reaping testifies to the sowing. Here no pretense is tolerated. Men may deceive their fellow men and may receive praise and compensation for service which they have not rendered. But in nature there can be no deception. On the unfaithful husbandman the harvest passes sentence of condemnation. And in the highest sense this is true also in the spiritual realm. It is in appearance, not in reality, that evil succeeds. The child who plays truant from school, the youth who is slothful in his studies, the clerk or apprentice who fails of serving the interests of his employer, the man in any business or profession who is untrue to his highest responsibilities, may flatter himself that, so long as the wrong is concealed, he is gaining an advantage. But not so; he is cheating himself. The harvest of life is character, and it is this that determines destiny, both for this life and for the life to come.

The harvest is a reproduction of the seed sown. Every seed yields fruit after its kind. So it is with the traits of character we cherish. Selfishness, self-love, self-esteem, self-indulgence, reproduce themselves, and the end is wretchedness and ruin. "He that soweth to his flesh shall of the flesh reap corruption; but he that soweth to the Spirit shall of the Spirit reap life everlasting." Galatians 6:8. Love, sympathy, and kindness yield fruitage of blessing, a harvest that is imperishable.

In the harvest the seed is multiplied. A single grain of wheat, increased by repeated sowings, would cover a whole land with golden sheaves. So widespread may be the influence of a single life, of even a single act.

What deeds of love the memory of that alabaster box broken for Christ's anointing has through the long centuries prompted! What countless gifts that contribution, by a poor unnamed widow, of "two mites, which make a farthing" (Mark 12:42), has brought to the Saviour's cause!

Life Through Death

The lesson of seed sowing teaches liberality. "He which soweth sparingly shall reap also sparingly; and he which soweth bountifully shall reap also bountifully." 2 Corinthians 9:6.

The Lord says, "Blessed are ye that sow beside all waters." Isaiah 32:20. To sow beside all waters means to give wherever our help is needed. This will not tend to poverty. "He which soweth bountifully shall reap also bountifully." By casting it away the sower multiplies his seed. So by imparting we increase our blessings. God's promise assures a sufficiency, that we may continue to give.

More than this: as we impart the blessings of this life, gratitude in the recipient prepares the heart to receive spiritual truth, and a harvest is produced unto life everlasting.

By the casting of grain into the earth, the Saviour represents His sacrifice for us. "Except a corn of wheat fall into the ground and die." He says, "it abideth alone: but if it die, it bringeth forth much fruit." John 12:24. Only through the sacrifice of Christ, the Seed, could fruit be brought forth for the kingdom of God. In accordance with the law of the vegetable kingdom, life is the result of His death.

So with all who bring forth fruit as workers together with Christ: self-love, self-interest, must perish; the life must be cast into the furrow of the world's need. But the law of self-sacrifice is the law of self-preservation. The husbandman preserves his grain by casting it away. So the life that will be preserved is the life that is freely given in service to God and man.

The seed dies, to spring forth into new life. In this we are taught the lesson of the resurrection. Of the human body laid away to molder in the grave, God has said: "It is sown in corruption; it is raised in incorruption: it is sown in dishonor; it is raised in glory: it is sown in weakness; it is raised in power." 1 Corinthians 15:42, 43.

As parents and teachers try to teach these lessons, the work should be made practical. Let the children themselves prepare the soil and sow the seed. As they work, the parent or teacher can explain the garden of the heart, with the good or bad seed sown there, and that as the garden must be prepared for the natural seed, so the heart must be prepared for the seed of truth. As the seed is cast into the ground, they can teach the lesson of Christ's death; and as the blade springs up, the truth of the resurrection. As the plant grows, the correspondence between the natural and the spiritual sowing may be continued.

The youth should be instructed in a similar way. From the tilling of the soil, lessons may constantly be learned. No one settles upon a raw piece of land with the expectation that it will at once yield a harvest. Diligent, persevering labor must be put forth in the preparation of the soil, the sowing of the seed, and the culture of the crop. So it must be in the spiritual sowing. The garden of the heart must be cultivated. The soil must be broken up by repentance. The evil growths that choke the good grain must be uprooted. As soil once overgrown with thorns can be reclaimed only by diligent labor, so the evil tendencies of the heart can be overcome only by earnest effort in the name and strength of Christ.

In the cultivation of the soil the thoughtful worker will find that treasures little dreamed of are opening up before him. No one can succeed in agriculture or gardening without attention to the laws involved. The special needs of every variety of plant must be studied. Different varieties require different soil and cultivation, and compliance with the laws governing each is the condition of success. The attention required in transplanting, that not even a root fiber shall be crowded or misplaced, the care of the young plants, the pruning and watering, the shielding from frost at night and sun by day, keeping out weeds, disease, and insect pests, the training and arranging, not only teach important lessons concerning the development of character, but the work itself is a means of development. In cultivating carefulness, patience, attention to detail, obedience to law, it imparts a most essential training. The constant contact with the mystery of life and the loveliness of nature, as well as the tenderness called forth in ministering to these beautiful objects of God's creation, tends to quicken the mind and refine and elevate the character; and the lessons taught prepare the worker to deal more successfully with other minds.

12
Other Object Lessons

"Whoso is wise, and will observe these things, even they shall understand the loving-kindness of the Lord."

God's healing power runs all through nature. If a tree is cut, if a human being is wounded or breaks a bone, nature begins at once to repair the injury. Even before the need exists, the healing agencies are in readiness; and as soon as a part is wounded, every energy is bent to the work of restoration. So it is in the spiritual realm. Before sin created the need, God had provided the remedy. Every soul that yields to temptation is wounded, bruised, by the adversary; but whenever there is sin, there is the Saviour. It is Christ's work "to heal the brokenhearted, to preach deliverance to the captives, . . . to set at liberty them that are bruised." Luke 4:18.

In this work we are to co-operate. "If a man be overtaken in a fault, . . . restore such an one." Galatians 6:1. The word here translated "restore" means to put in joint, as a dislocated bone. How suggestive the figure! He who falls into error or sin is thrown out of relation to everything about him. He may realize his error, and be filled with remorse; but he cannot recover himself. He is in confusion and perplexity, worsted and helpless. He is to be reclaimed, healed, re-established. "Ye which are spiritual, restore such an one." Only the love that flows from the heart of Christ can heal. Only he in whom that love flows, even as the sap in the tree or the blood in the body, can restore the wounded soul.

Love's agencies have wonderful power, for they are divine. The soft answer that "turneth away wrath," the love that "suffereth long, and is kind," the charity that "covereth a multitude of sins" (Proverbs 15:1; 1 Corinthians 13:4, R.V.; 1 Peter 4:8, R.V.)—would we learn the lesson, with what power for healing would our lives be gifted! How life would be transformed, and the earth become a very likeness and foretaste of heaven!

These precious lessons may be so simply taught as to be understood, even by little children. The heart of the child is tender and easily impressed; and when we who are older become "as little children" (Matthew 18:3); when we learn the simplicity and gentleness and tender love of the Saviour, we shall not find it difficult to touch the hearts of the little ones, and teach them love's ministry of healing.

Perfection exists in the least as well as in the greatest of the works of God. The hand that hung the worlds in space is the hand that fashions the flowers of the field. Examine under the microscope the smallest and commonest of wayside blossoms, and note in all its parts the exquisite beauty and completeness. So in the humblest lot true excellence may be found; the commonest tasks, wrought with loving faithfulness, are beautiful in God's sight. Conscientious attention to the little things will make us workers together with Him, and win for us His commendation who seeth and knoweth all.

The rainbow spanning the heavens with its arch of light is a token of "the everlasting covenant between God and every living creature." Genesis 9:16. And the rainbow encircling the throne on high is also a token to God's children of His covenant of peace.

As the bow in the cloud results from the union of sunshine and shower, so the bow above God's throne represents the union of His mercy and His justice. To the sinful but repentant soul God says, Live thou; "I have found a ransom." Job 33:24.

"As I have sworn that the waters of Noah should no more go over the earth; so have I sworn that I would not be wroth with thee, nor rebuke thee. For the mountains shall depart, and the hills be removed; but My kindness shall not depart from thee, neither shall the covenant of My peace be removed, saith the Lord that hath mercy on thee." Isaiah 54:9, 10.

The Message of the Stars

The stars also have a message of good cheer for every human being. In those hours that come to all, when the heart is faint and temptation presses sore; when obstacles seem insurmountable, life's aims impossible of achievement, its fair promises like apples of Sodom; where, then, can such courage and steadfastness be found as in that lesson which God has bidden us learn from the stars in their untroubled course?

"Lift up your eyes on high, and behold who hath created these things, that bringeth out their host by number: He calleth them all by names by the greatness of His might, for that He is strong in power; not one faileth. Why sayest thou, O Jacob, and speakest, O Israel, My way is hid from the Lord, and my judgment is passed over from my God? Hast thou not known? hast thou not heard, that the everlasting God, the Lord, the Creator of the ends of the earth, fainteth not, neither is weary? there is no searching of His understanding. He giveth power to the faint; and to them that have no might He increaseth strength." "Fear thou not; for I am with thee: be not dismayed for I am Thy God: I will strengthen thee; yea, I will help thee; yea, I will uphold thee with the right hand of My righteousness." "I the Lord thy God will hold thy right hand, saying unto thee, Fear not; I will help thee." Isaiah 40:26-29; 41:10, 13.

The palm tree, beaten by the scorching sun and the fierce sandstorm, stands green and flourishing and fruitful in the midst of the desert. Its roots are fed by living springs. Its crown of verdure is seen afar over the parched, desolate plain; and the traveler, ready to die, urges his failing steps to the cool shade and the life-giving water.

The tree of the desert is a symbol of what God means the life of His children in this world to be. They are to guide weary souls, full of unrest, and ready to perish in the desert of sin, to the living water. They are to point their fellow men to Him who gives the invitation, "If any man thirst, let him come unto Me, and drink." John 7:37.

The wide, deep river, that offers a highway for the traffic and travel of nations, is valued as a world-wide benefit; but what of the little rills that help to form this noble stream? Were it not for them, the river would disappear. Upon them its very existence depends. So men called to lead in some great work are honored as if its success were due to them alone; but that success required the faithful co-operation of humbler workers almost without number—workers of whom the world knows nothing. Tasks uncommended, labor without recognition, is the lot of most of the world's toilers. And in such a lot many are filled with discontent. They feel that life is wasted. But the little rill that makes its noiseless way through grove and meadow, bearing health and fertility and beauty, is as useful in its way as the broad river. And in contributing to the river's life, it helps achieve that which alone it could never have accomplished.

The lesson in one needed by many. Talent is too much idolized, and station too much coveted. There are too many who will do nothing unless they are recognized as leaders; too many who must receive praise, or they have no interest to labor. What we need to learn is faithfulness in making the utmost use of the powers and opportunities we have, and contentment in the lot to which Heaven assigns us.

A Lesson of Trust

"Ask now the beasts, and they shall teach thee; and the fowls of the air, and they shall tell thee: . . . and the fishes of the sea shall declare unto thee." "Go to the ant; . . . consider her ways." "Behold the birds." "Consider the ravens." Job 12:7, 8; Proverbs 6:6; Matthew 6:26, R.V.; Luke 12:24.

We are not merely to tell the child about these creatures of God. The animals themselves are to be his teachers. The ants teach lessons of patient industry, of perseverance in surmounting obstacles, of providence for the future. And the birds are teachers of the sweet lesson of trust. Our heavenly Father provides for them; but they must gather the food, they must build their nests and rear their young. Every moment they are exposed to enemies that seek to destroy them. Yet how cheerily they go about their work! how full of joy are their little songs!

How beautiful the psalmist's description of God's care for the creatures of the woods—

> "The high hills are a refuge for the wild goats;
> And the rocks for the conies."
>
> Psalm 104:18.

He sends the springs to run among the hills, where the birds have their habitation, and "sing among the branches." Psalm 104:12. All the creatures of the woods and hills are a part of His great household. He opens His hand, and satisfies "the desire of every living thing." Psalm 145:16.

The eagle of the Alps is sometimes beaten down by the tempest into the narrow defiles of the mountains. Storm clouds shut in this mighty bird of the forest, their dark masses separating her from the sunny heights where she has made her home. Her efforts to escape seem fruitless. She dashes to and fro, beating the air with her strong wings, and waking the mountain echoes with her cries. At length, with a note of triumph, she darts upward, and, piercing the clouds, is once more in the clear sunlight, with the darkness and tempest far beneath. So we may be surrounded with difficulties, discouragement, and darkness. Falsehood, calamity, injustice, shut us in. There are clouds that we cannot dispel. We battle with circumstances in vain. There is one, and but one, way of escape. The mists and fogs cling to the earth; beyond the clouds God's light is shining. Into the sunlight of His presence we may rise on the wings of faith.

Many are the lessons that may thus be learned. Self-reliance, from the tree that, growing alone on plain or mountainside, strikes down its roots deep into the earth, and in its rugged strength defies the tempest. The power of early influence, from the gnarled, shapeless trunk, bent as a sapling, to which no earthly power can afterward restore its lost symmetry. The secret of a holy life, from the water lily, that, on the bosom of some slimy pool, surrounded by weeds and rubbish, strikes down its channeled stem to the pure sands beneath, and, drawing thence its life, lifts up its fragrant blossoms to the light in spotless purity.

Thus while the children and youth gain a knowledge of facts from teachers and textbooks, let them learn to draw lessons and discern truth for themselves. In their gardening, question them as to what they learn from the care of their plants. As they look on a beautiful landscape, ask them why God clothed the fields and woods with such lovely and varied hues. Why was not all colored a somber brown? When they gather the flowers, lead them to think why He spared us the beauty of these wanderers from Eden. Teach them to notice the evidences everywhere manifest in nature of God's thought for us, the wonderful adaptation of all things to our need and happiness.

He alone who recognizes in nature his Father's handiwork, who in the richness and beauty of the earth reads the Father's handwriting—he alone learns from the things of nature their deepest lessons, and receives their highest ministry. Only he can fully appreciate the significance of hill and vale, river and sea, who looks upon them as an expression of the thought of God, a revelation of the Creator.

Many illustrations from nature are used by the Bible writers, and as we observe the things of the natural world, we shall be enabled, under the guiding of the Holy Spirit, more fully to understand the lessons of God's word. It is thus that nature becomes a key to the treasure house of the word.

Children should be encouraged to search out in nature the objects that illustrate Bible teachings, and to trace in the Bible the similitudes drawn from nature. They should search out, both in nature and in Holy Writ, every object representing Christ, and those also that He employed in illustrating truth. Thus may they learn to see Him in tree and vine, in lily and rose, in sun and star. They may learn to hear His voice in the song of birds, in the sighing of the trees, in the rolling thunder, and in the music of the sea. And every object in nature will repeat to them His precious lessons.

To those who thus acquaint themselves with Christ, the earth will nevermore be a lonely and desolate place. It will be their Father's house, filled with the presence of Him who once dwelt among men.

The Bible as an Educator

***"When thou goest, it shall lead thee; when thou sleepest,
it shall keep thee; and when thou awakest,
it shall talk with thee."***

13
Mental and Spiritual Culture

"By knowledge shall the chambers be filled with all precious and pleasant riches."

For the mind and the soul, as well as for the body, it is God's law that strength is acquired by effort. It is exercise that develops. In harmony with this law, God has provided in His word the means for mental and spiritual development.

The Bible contains all the principles that men need to understand in order to be fitted either for this life or for the life to come. And these principles may be understood by all. No one with a spirit to appreciate its teaching can read a single passage from the Bible without gaining from it some helpful thought. But the most valuable teaching of the Bible is not to be gained by occasional or disconnected study. Its great system of truth is not so presented as to be discerned by the hasty or careless reader. Many of its treasures lie far beneath the surface, and can be obtained only by diligent research and continuous effort. The truths that go to make up the great whole must be searched out and gathered up, "here a little, and there a little." Isaiah 28:10.

When thus searched out and brought together, they will be found to be perfectly fitted to one another. Each Gospel is a supplement to the others, every prophecy an explanation of another, every truth a development of some other truth. The types of the Jewish economy are made plain by the gospel. Every principle in the word of God has its place, every fact its bearing. And the complete structure, in design and execution, bears testimony to its Author. Such a structure no mind but that of the Infinite could conceive or fashion.

In searching out the various parts and studying their relationship, the highest faculties of the human mind are called into intense activity. No one can engage in such study without developing mental power.

And not alone in searching out truth and bringing it together does the mental value of Bible study consist. It consists also in the effort required to grasp the themes presented. The mind occupied with commonplace matters only, becomes dwarfed and enfeebled. If never tasked to comprehend grand and far-reaching truths, it after a time loses the power of growth. As a safeguard against this degeneracy, and a stimulus to development, nothing else can equal the study of God's word. As a means of intellectual training, the Bible is more effective than any other book, or all other books combined. The greatness of its themes, the dignified simplicity of its utterances, the beauty of its imagery, quicken and uplift the thoughts as nothing else can. No other study can impart such mental power as does the effort to grasp the stupendous truths of revelation. The mind thus brought in contact with the thoughts of the Infinite cannot but expand and strengthen.

And even greater is the power of the Bible in the development of the spiritual nature. Man, created for fellowship with God, can only in such fellowship find his real life and development. Created to find in God his highest joy, he can find in nothing else that which can quiet the cravings of the heart, can satisfy the hunger and thirst of the soul. He who with sincere and teachable spirit studies God's word, seeking to comprehend its truths, will be brought in touch with its Author; and, except by his own choice, there is no limit to the possibilities of his development.

In its wide range of style and subjects the Bible has something to interest every mind and appeal to every heart. In its pages are found history the most ancient; biography the truest to life; principles of government for the control of the state, for the regulation of the household—principles that human wisdom has never equaled. It contains philosophy the most profound, poetry the sweetest and the most sublime, the most impassioned and the most pathetic. Immeasurably superior in value to the productions of any human author are the Bible writings, even when thus considered; but of infinitely wider scope, of infinitely greater value, are they when viewed in their relation to the grand central thought. Viewed in the light of this thought, every topic has a new significance. In the most simply stated truths are involved principles that are as high as heaven and that compass eternity.

The central theme of the Bible, the theme about which every other in the whole book clusters, is the redemption plan, the restoration in human soul of the image of God. From the first intimation of hope in the sentence pronounced in Eden to that last glorious promise of the Revelation, "They shall see His face; and His name shall be in their foreheads" (Revelation 22:4), the burden of every book and every passage of the Bible is the unfolding of this wondrous theme—man's uplifting—the power of God, "which giveth us the victory through our Lord Jesus Christ." 1 Corinthians 15:57.

He who grasps this thought has before him an infinite field for study. He has the key that will unlock to him the whole treasure house of God's word.

The science of redemption is the science of all sciences; the science that is the study of the angels and of all the intelligences of the unfallen worlds; the science that engages the attention of our Lord and Saviour; the science that enters into the purpose brooded in the mind of the Infinite—"kept in silence through times eternal" (Romans 16:25, R.V.); the science that will be the study of God's redeemed throughout endless ages. This is the highest study in which it is possible for man to engage. As no other study can, it will quicken the mind and uplift the soul.

"The excellency of knowledge is, that wisdom giveth life to them that have it." "The words that I speak unto you," said Jesus, "they are spirit, and they are life." "This is life eternal, that they should know Thee the only true God, and Him whom Thou didst send." Ecclesiastes 7:12; John 6:63; 17:3, R.V.

The creative energy that called the worlds into existence is in the word of God. This word imparts power; it begets life. Every command is a promise; accepted by the will, received into the soul, it brings with it the life of the Infinite One. It transforms the nature and re-creates the soul in the image of God.

The life thus imparted is in like manner sustained. "By every word that proceedeth out of the mouth of God" (Matthew 4:4) shall man live.

The mind, the soul, is built up by that upon which it feeds; and it rests with us to determine upon what it shall be fed. It is within the power of everyone to choose the topics that shall occupy the thoughts and shape the character. Of every human being privileged with access to the Scriptures, God says, "I have written to him the great things of My law." "Call unto Me, and I will answer thee, and show thee great and mighty things, which thou knowest not." Hosea 8:12; Jeremiah 33:3.

With the word of God in his hands, every human being, wherever his lot in life may be cast, may have such companionship as he shall choose. In its pages he may hold converse with the noblest and best of the human race, and may listen to the voice of the Eternal as He speaks with men. As he studies and meditates upon the themes into which "the angels desire to look" (1 Peter 1:12), he may have their companionship. He may follow the steps of the heavenly Teacher, and listen to His words as when He taught on mountain and plain and sea. He may dwell in this world in the atmosphere of heaven, imparting to earth's sorrowing and tempted ones thoughts of hope and longings for holiness; himself coming closer and still closer into fellowship with the Unseen; like him of old who walked with God, drawing nearer and nearer the threshold of the eternal world, until the portals shall open, and he shall enter there. He will find himself no stranger. The voices that will greet him are the voices of the holy ones, who, unseen, were on earth his companions —voices that here he learned to distinguish and to love. He who through the word of God has lived in fellowship with heaven, will find himself at home in heaven's companionship.

14
Science and the Bible

"Who knoweth not in all these that the hand of the Lord hath wrought?"

Since the book of nature and the book of revelation bear the impress of the same master mind, they cannot but speak in harmony. By different methods, and in different languages, they witness to the same great truths. Science is ever discovering new wonders; but she brings from her research nothing that, rightly understood, conflicts with divine revelation. The book of nature and the written word shed light upon each other. They make us acquainted with God by teaching us something of the laws through which He works.

Inferences erroneously drawn from facts observed in nature have, however, led to supposed conflict between science and revelation; and in the effort to restore harmony, interpretations of Scripture have been adopted that undermine and destroy the force of the word of God. Geology has been thought to contradict the literal interpretation of the Mosaic record of the creation. Millions of years, it is claimed, were required for the evolution of the earth from chaos; and in order to accommodate the Bible to this supposed revelation of science, the days of creation are assumed to have been vast, indefinite periods, covering thousands or even millions of years.

Such a conclusion is wholly uncalled for. The Bible record is in harmony with itself and with the teaching of nature. Of the first day employed in the work of creation is given the record, "The evening and the morning were the first day." Genesis 1:5. And the same in substance is said of each of the first six days of creation week. Each of these periods Inspiration declares to have been a day consisting of evening and morning, like every other day since that time. In regard to the work of creation itself the divine testimony is, "He spake, and it was done; He commanded, and it stood fast." Psalm 33:9. With Him who could thus call into existence unnumbered worlds, how long a time would be required for the evolution of the earth from chaos? In order to account for His works, must we do violence to His word?

It is true that remains found in the earth testify to the existence of men, animals, and plants much larger than any now known. These are regarded as proving the existence of vegetable and animal life prior to the time of the Mosaic record. But concerning these things Bible history furnishes ample explanation. Before the Flood the development of vegetable and animal life was immeasurably superior to that which has since been known. At the Flood the surface of the earth was broken up, marked changes took place, and in the re-formation of the earth's crust were preserved many evidences of the life previously existing. The vast forests buried in the earth at the time of the Flood, and since changed to coal, form the extensive coal fields, and yield the supplies of oil that minister to our comfort and convenience today. These things, as they are brought to light, are so many witnesses mutely testifying to the truth of the word of God.

Akin to the theory concerning the evolution of the earth is that which attributes to an ascending line of germs, mollusks, and quadrupeds the evolution of man, the crowning glory of the creation.

When consideration is given to man's opportunities for research; how brief his life; how limited his sphere of action; how restricted his vision; how frequent and how great the errors in his conclusions, especially as concerns the events thought to antedate Bible history; how often the supposed deductions of science are revised or cast aside; with what readiness the assumed period of the earth's development is from time to time increased or diminished by millions of years; and how the theories advanced by different scientists conflict with one another—considering all this, shall we, for the privilege of tracing our descent from germs and mollusks and apes, consent to cast away that statement of Holy Writ, so grand in its simplicity, "God created man in His own image, in the image of God created He him"? Genesis 1:27. Shall we reject that genealogical record—prouder than any treasured in the courts of kings—"which was the son of Adam, which was the son of God"? Luke 3:38.

Rightly understood, both the revelations of science and the experiences of life are in harmony with the testimony of Scripture to the constant working of God in nature.

In the hymn recorded by Nehemiah, the Levites sang, "Thou, even Thou, art Lord alone; Thou hast made heaven, the heaven of heavens, with all their host, the earth, and all things that are therein, the seas, and all that is therein, and Thou preservest them all." Nehemiah 9:6.

As regards this earth, Scripture declares the work of creation to have been completed. "The works were finished from the foundation of the world." Hebrews 4:3. But the power of God is still exercised in upholding the objects of His creation. It is not because the mechanism once set in motion continues to act by its own inherent energy that the pulse beats, and breath follows breath. Every breath, every pulsation of the heart, is an evidence of the care of Him in whom we live and move and have our being. From the smallest insect to man, every living creature is daily dependent upon His providence.

"These wait all upon Thee. . . .
That Thou givest them they gather:
Thou openest Thine hand, they are filled with good.
Thou hidest Thy face, they are troubled:
Thou takest away their breath, they die,
And return to their dust.
Thou sendest forth Thy Spirit, they are created:
And Thou renewest the face of the earth."
Psalm 104:27-30.

"He stretcheth out the north over the empty place,
And hangeth the earth upon nothing.
He bindeth up the waters in His thick clouds;
And the cloud is not rent under them. . . .
He hath compassed the waters with bounds,
Until the day and night come to an end."
"The pillars of heaven tremble
And are astonished at His rebuke.
He stilleth the sea with His power. . . .
By His Spirit the heavens are beauty;
His hand hath pierced the gliding serpent.
Lo, these are but the outskirts of His ways:
And how small a whisper do we hear of Him!
But the thunder of His power who can understand?"
Job 26:7-10; 26:11-14, R.V., margin.

"The Lord hath His way in the whirlwind and in the storm,
And the clouds are the dust of His feet."
Nahum 1:3.

The mighty power that works through all nature and sustains all things is not, as some men of science claim, merely an all-pervading principle, an actuating energy. God is a spirit; yet He is a personal being, for man was made in His image. As a personal being, God has revealed Himself in His Son. Jesus, the outshining of the Father's glory, "and the express image of His person" (Hebrews 1:3), was on earth found in fashion as a man. As a personal Savior He came to the world. As a personal Savior He ascended on high. As a personal Savior He intercedes in the heavenly courts. Before the throne of God in our behalf ministers "One like the Son of man." Daniel 7:13.

The apostle Paul, writing by the Holy Spirit, declares of Christ that "all things have been created through Him, and unto Him; and He is before all things, and in Him all things hold together." Colossians 1:16, 17, R.V., margin. The hand that sustains the worlds in space, the hand that holds in their orderly arrangement and tireless activity all things throughout the universe of God, is the hand that was nailed to the cross for us.

The greatness of God is to us incomprehensible. "The Lord's throne is in heaven" (Psalm 11:4); yet by His Spirit He is everywhere present. He has an intimate knowledge of, and a personal interest in, all the works of His hand.

"Who is like unto the Lord our God, who dwelleth on high,
Who humbleth Himself to behold the things that are in heaven,
and in the earth!"
"Whither shall I go from Thy Spirit?
Or whither shall I flee from Thy presence?
If I ascend up into heaven, Thou art there:
If I make my bed in the grave, behold, Thou art there.
"If I take the wings of the morning,
And dwell in the uttermost parts of the sea;
Even there shall Thy hand lead me,
And Thy right hand shall hold me."

Psalms 113:5, 6; 139:7-10.
(see Psalm 139:8, R.V.; Job 26:6, R.V., margin)

"Thou knowest my downsitting and mine uprising,
Thou understandest my thought afar off.
Thou searchest out my path and my lying down,
And art acquainted with all my ways. . . .
Thou hast beset me behind and before,
And laid Thine hand upon me.
Such knowledge is too wonderful for me;
It is high, I cannot attain unto it."

Psalm 139:2-6, R.V.

It was the Maker of all things who ordained the wonderful adaptation of means to end, of supply to need. It was He who in the material world provided that every desire implanted should be met. It was He who created the human soul, with its capacity for knowing and for loving. And He is not in Himself such as to leave the demands of the soul unsatisfied. No intangible principle, no impersonal essence or mere abstraction, can satisfy the needs and longings of human beings in this life of struggle with sin and sorrow and pain. It is not enough to believe in law and force, in things that have no pity, and never hear the cry for help. We need to know of an almighty arm that will hold us up, of an infinite Friend that pities us. We need to clasp a hand that is warm, to trust in a heart full of tenderness. And even so God has in His word revealed Himself.

He who studies most deeply into the mysteries of nature will realize most fully his own ignorance and weakness. He will realize that there are depths and heights which he cannot reach, secrets which he cannot penetrate, vast fields of truth lying before him unentered. He will be ready to say, with Newton, "I seem to myself to have been like a child on the seashore finding pebbles and shells, while the great ocean of truth lay undiscovered before me."

The deepest students of science are constrained to recognize in nature the working of infinite power. But to man's unaided reason, nature's teaching cannot but be contradictory and disappointing. Only in the light of revelation can it be read aright. "Through faith we understand." Hebrews 11:3.

"In the beginning God." Genesis 1:1. Here alone can the mind in its eager questioning, fleeing as the dove to the ark, find rest. Above, beneath, beyond, abides Infinite Love, working out all things to accomplish "the good pleasure of His goodness." 2 Thessalonians 1:11.

"The invisible things of Him since the creation of the world are . . . perceived through the things that are made, even His everlasting power and divinity. Romans 1:20, R.V. But their testimony can be understood only through the aid of the divine Teacher. "What man knoweth the things of a man, save the spirit of man which is in him? even so the things of God knoweth no man, but the Spirit of God." 1 Corinthians 2:11.

"When He, the Spirit of truth, is come, He will guide you into all truth." John 16:13. Only by the aid of that Spirit who in the beginning "was brooding upon the face of the waters;" of that Word by whom "all things were made;" of that "true Light, which lighteth every man that cometh into the world," can the testimony of science be rightly interpreted. Only by their guidance can its deepest truths be discerned.

Only under the direction of the Omniscient One shall we, in the study of His works, be enabled to think His thoughts after Him.

15
Business Principles and Methods

"He that walketh uprightly walketh surely."

There is no branch of legitimate business for which the Bible does not afford an essential preparation. Its principles of diligence, honesty, thrift, temperance, and purity are the secret of true success. These principles, as set forth in the book of Proverbs, constitute a treasury of practical wisdom. Where can the merchant, the artisan, the director of men in any department of business, find better maxims for himself or for his employees than are found in these words of the wise man:

"Seest thou a man diligent in his business? he shall stand before kings; he shall not stand before mean men." Proverbs 22:29.

"In all labor there is profit: but the talk of the lips tendeth only to penury." Proverbs 14:23.

"The soul of the sluggard desireth, and hath nothing." "The drunkard and the glutton shall come to poverty: and drowsiness shall clothe a man with rags." Proverbs 13:4; 23:21.

"A talebearer revealeth secrets: therefore meddle not with him that flattereth with his lips." Proverbs 20:19.

"He that hath knowledge spareth his words;" but "every fool will be meddling." Proverbs 17:27; 20:3.

"Go not in the way of evil men;" "can one go upon hot coals, and his feet not be burned?" Proverbs 4:14; 6:28.

"He that walketh with wise men shall be wise." Proverbs 13:20.

"A man that hath friends must show himself friendly." Proverbs 18:24.

The whole circle of our obligation to one another is covered by that word of Christ's, "Whatsoever ye would that men should do to you, do ye even so to them." Matthew 7:12.

How many a man might have escaped financial failure and ruin by heeding the warnings, so often repeated and emphasized in the Scriptures:

"He that maketh haste to be rich shall not be innocent." Proverbs 28:20.

"Wealth gotten in haste shall be diminished: but he that gathereth by labor shall have increase." Proverbs 13:11, R.V., margin.

"The getting of treasures by a lying tongue is a vanity tossed to and fro of them that seek death." Proverbs 21:6.

"The borrower is servant to the lender." Proverbs 22:7.

"He that is surety for a stranger shall smart for it: and he that hateth suretyship is sure." Proverbs 11:15.

"Remove not the old landmark; and enter not into the fields of the fatherless: for their Redeemer is mighty; He shall plead their cause with thee." "He that oppresseth the poor to increase his riches, and he that giveth to the rich, shall surely come to want." "Whoso diggeth a pit shall fall therein: and he that rolleth a stone, it will return upon him." Proverbs 23:10, 11; 22:16; 26:27.

These are principles with which are bound up the well-being of society, of both secular and religious associations. It is these principles that give security to property and life. For all that makes confidence and co-operation possible, the world is indebted to the law of God, as given in His word, and as still traced, in lines often obscure and well-nigh obliterated, in the hearts of men.

The psalmist's words, "The law of Thy mouth is better unto me than thousands of gold and silver" (Psalm 119:72), state that which is true from other than a religious point of view. They state an absolute truth and one that is recognized in the business world. Even in this age of passion for money getting, when competition is so sharp and methods are so unscrupulous, it is still widely acknowledged that, for a young man starting in life, integrity, diligence, temperance, purity, and thrift constitute a better capital than any amount of mere money.

Yet even of those who appreciate the value of these qualities and acknowledge the Bible as their source, there are but few who recognize the principle upon which they depend.

That which lies at the foundation of business integrity and of true success is the recognition of God's ownership. The Creator of all things, He is the original proprietor. We are His stewards. All that we have is a trust from Him, to be used according to His direction.

This is an obligation that rests upon every human being. It has to do with the whole sphere of human activity. Whether we recognize it or not, we are stewards, supplied from God with talents and facilities, and placed in the world to do a work appointed by Him.

To every man is given "his work" (Mark 13:34), the work for which his capabilities adapt him, the work which will result in greatest good to himself and to his fellow men, and in greatest honor to God.

Thus our business or calling is a part of God's great plan, and, so long as it is conducted in accordance with His will, He Himself is responsible for the results. "Laborers together with God" (1 Corinthians 3:9), our part is faithful compliance with His directions. Thus there is no place for anxious care. Diligence, fidelity, caretaking, thrift, and discretion are called for. Every faculty is to be exercised to its highest capacity. But the dependence will be, not on the successful outcome of our efforts, but on the promise of God. The word that fed Israel in the desert, and sustained Elijah through the time of famine, has the same power today. "Be not anxious, saying, What shall we eat? or, What shall we drink? . . . Seek ye first the kingdom of God, and His righteousness; and all these things shall be added unto you." Matthew 6:31-33.

He who gives men power to get wealth has with the gift bound up an obligation. Of all that we acquire He claims a specified portion. The tithe is the Lord's. "All the tithe of the land, whether of the seed of the land, or of the fruit of the tree," "the tithe of the herd, or of the flock, . . . shall be holy unto the Lord." Leviticus 27:30, 32. The pledge made by Jacob at Bethel shows the extent of the obligation. "Of all that Thou shalt give me," he said, "I will surely give the tenth unto Thee." Genesis 28:22.

"Bring ye all the tithes into the storehouse" (Malachi 3:10), is God's command. No appeal is made to gratitude or to generosity. This is a matter of simple honesty. The tithe is the Lord's; and He bids us return to Him that which is His own.

"It is required in stewards, that a man be found faithful." 1 Corinthians 4:2. If honesty is an essential principle of business life, must we not recognize our obligation to God—the obligation that underlies every other?

By the terms of our stewardship we are placed under obligation, not only to God, but to man. To the infinite love of the Redeemer every human being is indebted for the gifts of life. Food and raiment and shelter, body and mind and soul—all are the purchase of His blood. And by the obligation of gratitude and service thus imposed, Christ has bound us to our fellow men. He bids us, "By love serve one another." Galatians 5:13. "Inasmuch as ye have done it unto one of the least of these My brethren, ye have done it unto Me." Matthew 25:40.

"I am debtor," Paul declares, "both to the Greeks, and to the barbarians; both to the wise, and to the unwise." Romans 1:14. So also are we. By all that has blessed our life above others, we are placed under obligation to every human being whom we might benefit.

These truths are not for the closet more than for the counting room. The goods that we handle are not our own, and never can this fact safely be lost sight of. We are but stewards, and on the discharge of our obligation to God and man depend both the welfare of our fellow beings and our own destiny for this life and for the life to come.

"There is that scattereth, and yet increaseth; and there is that withholdeth more than is meet, but it tendeth to poverty." "Cast thy bread upon the waters: for thou shalt find it after many days." "The liberal soul shall be made fat: and he that watereth shall be watered also himself." Proverbs 11:24, 25; Ecclesiastes 11:1.

"Labor not to be rich. . . . Wilt thou set thine eyes upon that which is not? for riches certainly make themselves wings; they fly away as an eagle toward heaven." Proverbs 23:4, 5.

"Give, and it shall be given unto you; good measure, pressed down, and shaken together, and running over, shall men give into your bosom. For with the same measure that ye mete withal it shall be measured to you again." Luke 6:38.

"Honor the Lord with thy substance, and with the first fruits of all thine increase: so shall thy barns be filled with plenty, and thy presses shall burst out with new wine." Proverbs 3:9, 10.

"Bring ye all the tithes into the storehouse, that there may be meat in Mine house, and prove Me now herewith, saith the Lord of hosts, if I will not open you the windows of heaven, and pour you out a blessing, that there shall not be room enough to receive it. And I will rebuke the devourer for your sakes, and he shall not destroy the fruits of your ground; neither shall your vine cast her fruit before the time in the field. . . . And all nations shall call you blessed: for ye shall be a delightsome land." Malachi 3:10-12.

"If ye walk in My statutes, and keep My commandments, and do them; then I will give you rain in due season, and the land shall yield her increase, and the trees of the field shall yield their fruit. And your threshing shall reach unto the vintage, and the vintage shall reach unto the sowing time: and ye shall eat your bread to the full, and dwell in your land safely. And I will give peace in the land, . . . and none shall make you afraid." Leviticus 26:3-6.

"Seek judgment, relieve the oppressed, judge the fatherless, plead for the widow." "Blessed is he that considereth the poor: the Lord will deliver him in time of trouble. The Lord will preserve him, and keep him alive; and he shall be blessed upon the earth: and Thou wilt not deliver him unto the will of his enemies." "He that hath pity upon the poor lendeth unto the Lord; and that which he hath given will He pay him again." Isaiah 1:17; Psalm 41:1, 2; Proverbs 19:17.

He who makes this investment lays up double treasure. Besides that which, however wisely improved, he must leave at last, he is amassing wealth for eternity—that treasure of character which is the most valuable possession of earth or heaven.

Honest Business Dealings

"The Lord knoweth the days of the upright: and their inheritance shall be forever. They shall not be ashamed in the evil time: and in the days of famine they shall be satisfied." Psalm 37:18, 19.

"He that walketh uprightly, and worketh righteousness, and speaketh the truth in his heart. . . . He that sweareth to his own hurt, and changeth not;" "he that despiseth the gain of oppressions, that shaketh his hands from holding of bribes, . . . and shutteth his eyes from seeing evil; he shall dwell on high: . . . bread shall be given him; his waters shall be sure. Thine eyes shall see the King in His beauty: they shall behold the land that is very far off." Psalm 15:2-4; Isaiah 33:15-17.

God has given in His word a picture of a prosperous man—one whose life was in the truest sense a success, a man whom both heaven and earth delighted to honor. Of his experiences Job himself says:

"In the ripeness of my days,
When the secret of God was upon my tent;
When the Almighty was yet with me,
And my children were about me; . . .
When I went forth to the gate unto the city,
When I prepared my seat in the broad place [margin],
The young men saw me and hid themselves,
And the aged rose up and stood;
The princes refrained talking,
And laid their hand on their mouth;
The voice of the nobles was hushed. . . .
"For when the ear heard me, then it blessed me;
And when the eye saw me, it gave witness unto me;
Because I delivered the poor that cried,
The fatherless also, and him [margin], that had none to help him.
"The blessing of him that was ready to perish came upon me;
And I caused the widow's heart to sing for joy.
I put on righteousness, and it clothed me:
My justice was as a robe and a diadem.
I was eyes to the blind,
And feet was I to the lame.
I was a father to the needy:
And the cause of him that I knew not I searched out."
"The stranger did not lodge in the street:
But I opened my doors to the traveler."
"Unto me men gave ear, and waited. . . .
And the light of my countenance they cast not down.
I chose out their way, and sat chief,
And dwelt as a king in the army,
As one that *comforteth the mourners*."
Job 29:4-16, R.V.; 31:32; 29:21-25.

"The blessing of the Lord, it maketh rich, and He addeth no sorrow with it." Proverbs 10:22.

"Riches and honor are with Me," declares Wisdom; "yea, durable riches and righteousness." Proverbs 8:18.

The Bible shows also the result of a departure from right principles in our dealing both with God and with one another. To those who are entrusted with His gifts but indifferent to His claims, God says:

"Consider your ways. Ye have sown much, and bring in little; ye eat, but ye have not enough; ye drink, but ye are not filled with drink; ye clothe you, but there is none warm; and he that earneth wages earneth wages to put it into a bag with holes. . . . Ye looked for much, and, lo, it came to little; and when ye brought it home, I did blow upon it." "When one came to an heap of twenty measures, there were but ten: when one came to the pressfat for to draw out fifty vessels out of the press, there were but twenty." "Why? saith the Lord of hosts. Because of Mine house that is waste." "Will a man rob God? Yet ye have robbed Me. But ye say, Wherein have we robbed Thee? In tithes and offerings." "Therefore the heaven over you is stayed from dew, and the earth is stayed from her fruit." Haggai 1:5-9; 2:16; Malachi 3:8; Haggai 1:10.

"Forasmuch therefore as your treading is upon the poor, . . . ye have built houses of hewn stone, but ye shall not dwell in them; ye have planted pleasant vineyards, but ye shall not drink wine of them." "The Lord shall send upon thee cursing, vexation, and rebuke, in all that thou settest thine hand unto." "Thy sons and thy daughters shall be given unto another, . . . and thine eyes shall look, and fail with longing for them all the day long: and there shall be no might in thine hand." Amos 5:11; Deuteronomy 28:20, 32.

"He that getteth riches, and not by right, shall leave them in the midst of his days, and at his end shall be a fool." Jeremiah 17:11.

The accounts of every business, the details of every transaction, pass the scrutiny of unseen auditors, agents of Him who never compromises with injustice, never overlooks evil, never palliates wrong.

"If thou seest the oppression of the poor, and violent perverting of judgment and justice, . . . marvel not at the matter: for He that is higher than the highest regardeth." "There is no darkness, nor shadow of death, where the workers of iniquity may hide themselves." Ecclesiastes 5:8, Job 34:22.

"They set their mouth against the heavens. . . . And they say, How doth God know? and is there knowledge in the Most High?" "These things hast thou done," God says, "and I kept silence; thou thoughtest that I was altogether such an one as thyself: but I will reprove thee, and set them in order before thine eyes," Psalms 73:9-11; 50:21.

"I turned, and lifted up mine eyes, and looked, and behold a flying roll. . . . This is the curse that goeth forth over the face of the whole earth: for everyone that stealeth shall be cut off as on this side according to it; and everyone that sweareth shall be cut off as on that side according to it. I will bring it forth, saith the Lord of hosts, and it shall enter into the house of the thief, and into the house of him that sweareth falsely by My name: and it shall remain in the midst of his house, and shall consume it with the timber thereof and the stones thereof." Zechariah 5:1-4.

Against every evildoer God's law utters condemnation. He may disregard that voice, he may seek to drown its warning, but in vain. It follows him. It makes itself heard. It destroys his peace. If unheeded, it pursues him to the grave. It bears witness against him at the judgement. A quenchless fire, it consumes at last soul and body.

"What shall it profit a man, if he shall gain the whole world, and lose his own soul? Or what shall a man give in exchange for his soul?" Mark 8:36, 37.

This is a question that demands consideration by every parent, every teacher, every student—by every human being, young or old. No scheme of business or plan of life can be sound or complete that embraces only the brief years of this present life and makes no provision for the unending future. Let the youth be taught to take eternity into their reckoning. Let them be taught to choose the principles and seek the possessions that are enduring—to lay up for themselves that "treasure in the heavens that faileth not, where no thief approacheth, neither moth corrupteth;" to make to themselves friends "by means of the mammon of unrighteousness," that when it shall fail, these may receive them "into the eternal tabernacles." Luke 12:33; 16:9, R.V.

All who do this are making the best possible preparation for life in this world. No man can lay up treasure in heaven without finding his life on earth thereby enriched and ennobled.

"Godliness is profitable unto all things, having promise of the life that now is, and of that which is to come." 1 Timothy 4:8.

16
Bible Biographies

"Who through faith subdued kingdoms, wrought righteousness, . . . out of weakness were made strong."

As an educator no part of the Bible is of greater value than are its biographies. These biographies differ from all others in that they are absolutely true to life. It is impossible for any finite mind to interpret rightly, in all things, the workings of another. None but He who reads the heart, who discerns the secret springs of motive and action, can with absolute truth delineate character, or give a faithful picture of a human life. In God's word alone is found such delineation.

No truth does the Bible more clearly teach than that what we do is the result of what we are. To a great degree the experiences of life are the fruition of our own thoughts and deeds.

"The curse causeless shall not come." Proverbs 26:2.

"Say ye to the righteous, that it shall be well with him. . . . Woe unto the wicked! it shall be ill with him: for the reward of his hands shall be given him." Isaiah 3: 10, 11.

"Hear, O earth: behold, I will bring evil upon this people, even the fruit of their thoughts." Jeremiah 6:19.

Terrible is this truth, and deeply should it be impressed. Every deed reacts upon the doer. Never a human being but may recognize, in the evils that curse his life, fruitage of his own sowing. Yet even thus we are not without hope.

To gain the birthright that was his already by God's promise, Jacob resorted to fraud, and he reaped the harvest in his brother's hatred. Through twenty years of exile he was himself wronged and defrauded, and was at last forced to find safety in flight; and he reaped a second harvest, as the evils of his own character were seen to crop out in his sons—all but too true a picture of the retributions of human life.

But God says: "I will not contend forever, neither will I be always wroth: for the spirit should fail before Me, and the souls which I have made. For the iniquity of his covetousness was I wroth, and smote him: I hid Me, and was wroth, and he went on frowardly in the way of his heart. I have seen his ways, and will heal him: I will lead him also, and restore comforts unto him and to his mourners. . . . Peace, peace to him that is far off, and to him that is near, saith the Lord; and I will heal him." Isaiah 57:16-19.

Jacob in his distress was not overwhelmed. He had repented, he had endeavored to atone for the wrong to his brother. And when threatened with death through the wrath of Esau, he sought help from God. "Yea, he had power over the Angel, and prevailed: he wept, and made supplication." "And He blessed him there." Hosea 12:4; Genesis 32:29. In the power of His might the forgiven one stood up, no longer the supplanter, but a prince with God. He had gained not merely deliverance from his outraged brother, but deliverance from himself. The power of evil in his own nature was broken; his character was transformed.

At eventide there was light. Jacob, reviewing his life-history, recognized the sustaining power of God—"the God which fed me all my life long unto this day, the Angel which redeemed me from all evil." Genesis 48:15, 16.

The same experience is repeated in the history of Jacob's sons—sin working retribution, and repentance bearing fruit of righteousness unto life.

God does not annul His laws. He does not work contrary to them. The work of sin He does not undo. But He transforms. Through His grace the curse works out blessing.

Of the sons of Jacob, Levi was one of the most cruel and vindictive, one of the two most guilty in the treacherous murder of the Shechemites. Levi's characteristics, reflected in his descendants, incurred for them the decree from God, "I will divide them in Jacob, and scatter them in Israel." Genesis 49:7. But repentance wrought reformation; and by their faithfulness to God amidst the apostasy of the other tribes, the curse was transformed into a token of highest honor.

"The Lord separated the tribe of Levi, to bear the ark of the covenant of the Lord, to stand before the Lord to minister unto Him, and to bless in His name." "My covenant was with him of life and peace; and I gave them to him for the fear wherewith he feared Me, and was afraid before My name. . . . He walked with Me in peace and equity, and did turn many away from iniquity." Deuteronomy 10:8; Malachi 2:5, 6.

The appointed ministers of the sanctuary, the Levites received no landed inheritance; they dwelt together in cities set apart for their use, and received their support from the tithes and the gifts and offerings devoted to God's service. They were the teachers of the people, guests at all their festivities, and everywhere honored as servants and representatives of God. To the whole nation was given the command: "Take heed to thyself that thou forsake not the Levite as long as thou livest upon the earth." "Levi hath no part nor inheritance with his brethren; the Lord is his inheritance." Deuteronomy 12:19; 10:9.

By Faith to Conquest

The truth that as a man "thinketh in his heart, so is he" (Proverbs 23:7), finds another illustration in Israel's experience. On the borders of Canaan the spies, returned from searching the country, made their report. The beauty and fruitfulness of the land were lost sight of through fear of the difficulties in the way of its occupation. The cities walled up to heaven, the giant warriors, the iron chariots, daunted their faith. Leaving God out of the question, the multitude echoed the decision of the unbelieving spies, "We be not able to go up against the people; for they are stronger than we." Numbers 13:31. Their words proved true. They were not able to go up, and they wore out their lives in the desert.

Two, however, of the twelve who had viewed the land, reasoned otherwise. "We are well able to overcome it" (Numbers 13:30), they urged, counting God's promise superior to giants, walled cities, or chariots of iron. For them their word was true. Though they shared with their brethren the forty years' wandering, Caleb and Joshua entered the Land of Promise. As courageous of heart as when with the hosts of the Lord he set out from Egypt, Caleb asked for and received as his portion the stronghold of the giants. In God's strength he drove out the Canaanites. The vineyards and olive groves where his feet had trodden became his possession. Though the cowards and rebels perished in the wilderness, the men of faith ate of the grapes of Eschol.

No truth does the Bible set forth in clearer light than the peril of even one departure from the right—peril both to the wrongdoer and to all whom his influence shall reach. Example has wonderful power; and when cast on the side of the evil tendencies of our nature, it becomes well-nigh irresistible.

The strongest bulwark of vice in our world is not the iniquitous life of the abandoned sinner or the degraded outcast; it is that life which otherwise appears virtuous, honorable, and noble, but in which one sin is fostered, one vice indulged. To the soul that is struggling in secret against some giant temptation, trembling upon the very verge of the precipice, such an example is one of the most powerful enticements to sin. He who, endowed with high conceptions of life and truth and honor, does yet willfully transgress one precept of God's holy law, has perverted his noble gifts into a lure to sin. Genius, talent, sympathy, even generous and kindly deeds, may thus become decoys of Satan to entice souls over the precipice of ruin.

This is why God has given so many examples showing the results of even one wrong act. From the sad story of that one sin which "brought death into the world and all our woe, with loss of Eden," to the record of him who for thirty pieces of silver sold the Lord of glory, Bible biography abounds in these examples, set up as beacons of warning at the byways leading from the path of life.

There is warning also in noting the results that have followed upon even once yielding to human weakness and error, the fruit of the letting go of faith.

By one failure of his faith, Elijah cut short his lifework. Heavy was the burden that he had borne in behalf of Israel; faithful had been his warnings against the national idolatry; and deep was his solicitude as during three years and a half of famine he watched and waited for some token of repentance. Alone he stood for God upon Mount Carmel. Through the power of faith, idolatry was cast down, and the blessed rain testified to the showers of blessing waiting to be poured upon Israel. Then in his weariness and weakness he fled before the threats of Jezebel and alone in the desert prayed that he might die. His faith had failed. The work he had begun he was not to complete. God bade him anoint another to be prophet in his stead.

But God had marked the heart service of His servant. Elijah was not to perish in discouragement and solitude in the wilderness. Not for him the descent to the tomb, but the ascent with God's angels to the presence of His glory.

These life records declare what every human being will one day understand—that sin can bring only shame and loss; that unbelief means failure; but that God's mercy reaches to the deepest depths; that faith lifts up the repenting soul to share the adoption of the sons of God.

The Discipline of Suffering

All who in this world render true service to God or man receive a preparatory training in the school of sorrow. The weightier the trust and the higher the service, the closer is the test and the more severe the discipline.

Study the experiences of Joseph and of Moses, of Daniel and of David. Compare the early history of David with the history of Solomon, and consider the results.

David in his youth was intimately associated with Saul, and his stay at court and his connection with the king's household gave him an insight into the cares and sorrows and perplexities concealed by the glitter and pomp of royalty. He saw of how little worth is human glory to bring peace to the soul. And it was with relief and gladness that he returned from the king's court to the sheepfolds and the flocks.

When by the jealousy of Saul driven a fugitive into the wilderness, David, cut off from human support, leaned more heavily upon God. The uncertainty and unrest of the wilderness life, its unceasing peril, its necessity for frequent flight, the character of the men who gathered to him there—"everyone that was in distress, and everyone that was in debt, and everyone that was discontented" (1 Samuel 22:2)—all rendered the more essential a stern self-discipline. These experiences aroused and developed power to deal with men, sympathy for the oppressed, and hatred of injustice. Through years of waiting and peril, David learned to find in God his comfort, his support, his life. He learned that only by God's power could he come to the throne; only in His wisdom could he rule wisely. It was through the training in the school of hardship and sorrow that David was able to make the record—though afterward marred with his great sin—that he "executed judgment and justice unto all his people." 2 Samuel 8:15.

The discipline of David's early experience was lacking in that of Solomon. In circumstances, in character, and in life, he seemed favored above all others. Noble in youth, noble in manhood, the beloved of his God, Solomon entered on a reign that gave high promise of prosperity and honor. Nations marveled at the knowledge and insight of the man to whom God had given wisdom. But the pride of prosperity brought separation from God. From the joy of divine communion Solomon turned to find satisfaction in the pleasures of sense. Of this experience he says:

"I made me great works; I builded me houses; I planted me vineyards: I made me gardens and orchards: . . . I got me servants and maidens: . . . I gathered me also silver and gold, and the peculiar treasure of kings and of the provinces: I gat me men singers and women singers, and the delights of the sons of men, as musical instruments, and that of all sorts. So I was great, and increased more than all that were before me in Jerusalem. . . . And whatsoever mine eyes desired I kept not from them, I withheld not my heart from any joy; for my heart rejoiced in all my labor. . . . Then I looked on all the works that my hands had wrought, and on the labor that I had labored to do: and, behold, all was vanity and vexation of spirit, and there was no profit under the sun. And I turned myself to behold wisdom, and madness, and folly: for what can the man do that cometh after the king? even that which hath been already done."

"I hated life. . . . Yea, I hated all my labor which I had taken under the sun." Ecclesiastes 2:4-12, 17, 18.

By his own bitter experience, Solomon learned the emptiness of a life that seeks in earthly things its highest good. He erected altars to heathen gods, only to learn how vain is their promise of rest to the soul.

In his later years, turning wearied and thirsting from earth's broken cisterns, Solomon returned to drink at the fountain of life. The history of his wasted years, with their lessons of warning, he by the Spirit of inspiration recorded for after generations. And thus, although the seed of his sowing was reaped by his people in harvests of evil, the lifework of Solomon was not wholly lost. For him at last the discipline of suffering accomplished its work.

But with such a dawning, how glorious might have been his life's day had Solomon in his youth learned the lesson that suffering had taught in other lives!

The Testing of Job

For those who love God, those who are "the called according to His purpose" (Romans 8:28), Bible biography has a yet higher lesson of the ministry of sorrow. "Ye are My witnesses, saith the Lord, that I am God" (Isaiah

43:12)—witnesses that He is good, and that goodness is supreme. "We are made a theater unto the world, both to angels, and to men." 1 Corinthians 4:9, margin.

Unselfishness, the principle of God's kingdom, is the principle that Satan hates; its very existence he denies. From the beginning of the great controversy he has endeavored to prove God's principles of action to be selfish, and he deals in the same way with all who serve God. To disprove Satan's claim is the work of Christ and of all who bear His name.

It was to give in His own life an illustration of unselfishness that Jesus came in the form of humanity. And all who accept this principle are to be workers together with Him in demonstrating it in practical life. To choose the right because it is right; to stand for truth at the cost of suffering and sacrifice—"this is the heritage of the servants of the Lord, and their righteousness is of Me, saith the Lord." Isaiah 54:17.

Very early in the history of the world is given the life record of one over whom this controversy of Satan's was waged.

Of Job, the patriarch of Uz, the testimony of the Searcher of hearts was, "There is none like him in the earth, a perfect and an upright man, one that feareth God, and escheweth evil."

Against this man, Satan brought scornful charge: "Doth Job fear God for nought? Hast Thou not made an hedge about him, and about his house, and about all that he hath on every side? . . . Put forth Thine hand now, and touch all that he hath;" "touch his bone and his flesh, and he will curse Thee to Thy face."

The Lord said unto Satan, "All that he hath is in thy power." "Behold, he is in thine hand; but save his life."

Thus permitted, Satan swept away all that Job possessed—flocks and herds, menservants and maidens, sons and daughters; and he "smote Job with sore boils from the sole of his foot unto his crown." Job 1:8-12; 2:5-7.

Still another element of bitterness was added to his cup. His friends, seeing in adversity but the retribution of sin, pressed on his bruised and burdened spirit their accusations of wrongdoing.

Seemingly forsaken of heaven and earth, yet holding fast his faith in God and his consciousness of integrity, in anguish and perplexity he cried:

> "My soul is weary of my life."
> "O that Thou wouldest hide me in the grave,
> That Thou wouldest keep me secret, until Thy wrath be past,
> That Thou wouldest appoint me a set time, and remember me!"
> Job 10:1; 14:13.

> "Behold, I cry out of wrong, but I am not heard:
> I cry for help, but there is no judgment. . . .
> He hath stripped me of my glory,

And taken the crown from my head. . . .
My kinsfolk have failed,
And my familiar friends have forgotten me. . .
They whom I loved are turned against me. . . .
Have pity upon me, have pity upon me, O ye my friends;
For the hand of God hath touched me."
"Oh that I knew where I might find Him,
That I might come even to His seat! . . .
Behold, I go forward, but He is not there;
And backward, but I cannot perceive Him:
On the left hand, where He doth work, but I cannot behold Him:
He hideth Himself on the right hand, that I cannot see Him.
But He knoweth the way that I take;
When He hath tried me, I shall come forth as gold."
"Though He slay me, yet will I trust in Him."
"I know that my Redeemer liveth,
And that He shall stand up at the last upon the earth:
And after my skin hath been destroyed, this shall be,
Even from my flesh shall I see God:
Whom I shall see for myself,
And mine eyes shall behold, and not as a stranger."
Job 19:7-21, R.V.; 23:3-10, R.V.; 13:15; 19:25-27, R.V., margin.

According to his faith, so was it unto Job. "When He hath tried me," he said, "I shall come forth as gold." Job 23:10. So it came to pass. By his patient endurance he vindicated his own character, and thus the character of Him whose representative he was. And "the Lord turned the captivity of Job: . . . also the Lord gave Job twice as much as he had before. . . . So the Lord blessed the latter end of Job more than his beginning." Job 42:10-12.

On the record of those who through self-abnegation have entered into the fellowship of Christ's sufferings, stand—one in the Old Testament and one in the New—the names of Jonathan and of John the Baptist.

Jonathan, by birth heir to the throne, yet knowing himself set aside by the divine decree; to his rival the most tender and faithful of friends, shielding David's life at the peril of his own; steadfast at his father's side through the dark days of his declining power, and at his side falling at the last—the name of Jonathan is treasured in heaven, and it stands on earth a witness to the existence and the power of unselfish love.

John the Baptist, at his appearance as the Messiah's herald, stirred the nation. From place to place his steps were followed by vast throngs of people of every rank and station. But when the One came to whom he had borne witness, all was changed. The crowds followed Jesus, and John's work seemed fast closing. Yet there was no wavering of his faith. "He must increase," he said, "but I must decrease." John 3:30.

Time passed, and the kingdom which John had confidently expected was not established. In Herod's dungeon, cut off from the life-giving air and the desert freedom, he waited and watched.

There was no display of arms, no rending of prison doors; but the healing of the sick, the preaching of the gospel, the uplifting of men's souls, testified to Christ's mission.

Alone in the dungeon, seeing whither his path, like his Master's, tended, John accepted the trust—fellowship with Christ in sacrifice. Heaven's messengers attended him to the grave. The intelligences of the universe, fallen and unfallen, witnessed his vindication of unselfish service.

And in all the generations that have passed since then, suffering souls have been sustained by the testimony of John's life. In the dungeon, on the scaffold, in the flames, men and women through centuries of darkness have been strengthened by the memory of him of whom Christ declared, "Among them that are born of women there hath not risen a greater." Matthew 11:11.

"And what shall I more say? for the time would fail me to tell of Gideon, and of Barak, and of Samson, and of Jephthah; . . . and Samuel, and of the prophets: who through faith subdued kingdoms, wrought righteousness, obtained promises, stopped the mouths of lions, quenched the violence of fire, escaped the edge of the sword, out of weakness were made strong, waxed valiant in fight, turned to flight the armies of the aliens.

"Women received their dead raised to life again: and others were tortured, not accepting deliverance; that they might obtain a better resurrection: and others had trial of cruel mockings and scourgings, yea, moreover of bonds and imprisonment: they were stoned, they were sawn asunder, were tempted, were slain with the sword: they wandered about in sheepskins and goatskins; being destitute, afflicted, tormented; (of whom the world was not worthy:) they wandered in deserts, and in mountains, and in dens and caves of the earth.

"And these all, having obtained a good report through faith, received not the promise: God having provided some better thing for us, that they without us should not be made perfect." Hebrews 11:32-40.

17
Poetry and Song

"Thy statutes have been my songs in the house of my pilgrimage."

The earliest as well as the most sublime of poetic utterances known to man are found in the Scriptures. Before the oldest of the world's poets had sung, the shepherd of Midian recorded those words of God to Job—in their majesty unequaled, unapproached, by the loftiest productions of human genius:

"Where wast thou when I laid the foundations of the earth? . . .
Or who shut up the sea with doors,
When it brake forth; . . .
When I made the cloud the garment thereof,
And thick darkness a swaddling band for it,
And prescribed for it My decree,
And set bars and doors,
And said, Hitherto shalt thou come, but no further;
And here shall thy proud waves be stayed?

"Hast thou commanded the morning since thy days began,
And caused the dayspring to know its place? . . .

"Hast thou entered into the springs of the sea?
Or hast thou walked in the recesses of the deep?
Have the gates of death been revealed unto thee?
Or hast thou seen the gates of the shadow of death?
Hast thou comprehended the breadth of the earth?
Declare, if thou knowest it all.

"Where is the way to the dwelling of light,
And as for darkness, where is the place thereof? . . .
"Hast thou entered the treasuries of the snow,
Or hast thou seen the treasuries of the hail? . . .
By what way is the light parted,
Or the east wind scattered upon the earth?
Who hath cleft a channel for the water flood,
Or a way for the lightning of the thunder;
To cause it to rain on a land where no man is;
On the wilderness, wherein there is no man;
To satisfy the waste and desolate ground;
And to cause the tender grass to spring forth?"

"Canst thou bind the sweet influences of Pleiades,
Or loose the bands of Orion?
Canst thou bring forth Mazzaroth in his season?
Or canst thou guide Arcturus with his sons?"

Job 38:4-27, R.V.; 38:31, 32.

For beauty of expression read also the description of springtime, from the Song of Songs:

"Lo, the winter is past,
The rain is over and gone;
The flowers appear on the earth;
The time of the singing of birds is come,
And the voice of the turtle is heard in our land;
The fig tree ripeneth her green figs,
And the vines are in blossom,
They give forth their fragrance.
Arise, my love, my fair one, and come away."
Song of Solomon 2:11-13, R.V.

And not inferior in beauty is Balaam's unwilling prophecy of blessing to Israel:

"From Aram hath Balak brought me,
The king of Moab from the mountains of the East:
Come, curse me Jacob,
And come, defy Israel.
How shall I curse, whom God hath not cursed?
And how shall I defy, whom the Lord hath not defied?
For from the top of the rocks I see him?
And from the hills I behold him:
Lo, it is a people that dwell alone,
And shall not be reckoned among the nations. . . .

"Behold, I have received commandment to bless:
And He hath blessed, and I cannot reverse it.
He hath not beheld iniquity in Jacob,
Neither hath He seen perverseness in Israel:
The Lord his God is with him,
And the shout of a King is among them. . . .
Surely there is no enchantment against Jacob,
Neither is there any divination against Israel:
Now shall it be said of Jacob and of Israel,
What hath God wrought!"

"He saith, which heareth the words of God,
Which seeth the vision of the Almighty: . . .
How goodly are thy tents, O Jacob,
Thy tabernacles, O Israel!
As valleys are they spread forth,
As gardens by the riverside,
As lignaloes which the Lord hath planted,
As cedar trees beside the waters."

"He hath said, which heard the words of God,
And knew the knowledge of the Most High: . . .
I shall see Him, but not now:
I shall behold Him, but not nigh:

There shall come a Star out of Jacob,
And a Scepter shall rise out of Israel. . . .
Out of Jacob shall come He that shall have dominion."
Numbers 23:7-23, R.V.; 24:4-6, R.V.; 24:16-19.

The melody of praise is the atmosphere of heaven; and when heaven comes in touch with the earth, there is music and song—"thanksgiving, and the voice of melody." Isaiah 51:3.

Above the new-created earth, as it lay, fair and unblemished, under the smile of God, "the morning stars sang together, and all the sons of God shouted for joy." Job 38:7. So human hearts, in sympathy with heaven, have responded to God's goodness in notes of praise. Many of the events of human history have been linked with song.

The earliest song recorded in the Bible from the lips of men was that glorious outburst of thanksgiving by the hosts of Israel at the Red Sea:

"I will sing unto the Lord, for He hath triumphed gloriously:
The horse and his rider hath He thrown into the sea.
The Lord is my strength and song,
And He is become my salvation:
This is my God, and I will praise Him;
My father's God, and I will exalt Him."

"Thy right hand, O Lord, is glorious in power,
Thy right hand, O Lord, dasheth in pieces the enemy. . . .
Who is like unto Thee, O Lord, among the gods?
Who is like Thee, glorious in holiness,
Fearful in praises, doing wonders?"

"The Lord shall reign for ever and ever. . . .
Sing ye to the Lord, for He hath triumphed gloriously."
Exodus 15:1, 2, 6-11, 18-21, R.V.

Great have been the blessings received by men in response to songs of praise. The few words recounting an experience of the wilderness journey of Israel have a lesson worthy of our thought:

"They went to Beer: that is the well whereof the Lord spake unto Moses, Gather the people together, and I will give them water." Numbers 21:16. "Then sang Israel this song:

"Spring up, O well; sing ye unto it:
The well, which the princes digged,
Which the nobles of the people delved,
With the scepter, and with their staves."
Numbers 21:17, 18, R.V.

How often in spiritual experience is this history repeated! how often by words of holy song are unsealed in the soul the springs of penitence and faith, of hope and love and joy!

It was with songs of praise that the armies of Israel went forth to the great deliverance under Jehoshaphat. To Jehoshaphat had come the tidings of threatened war. "There cometh a great multitude against thee," was the message, "the children of Moab, and the children of Ammon, and with them other beside." "And Jehoshaphat feared, and set himself to seek the Lord, and proclaimed a fast throughout all Judah. And Judah gathered themselves together, to ask help of the Lord: even out of all the cities of Judah they came to seek the Lord." And Jehoshaphat, standing in the temple court before his people, poured out his soul in prayer, pleading God's promise, with confession of Israel's helplessness. "We have no might against this great company that cometh against us," he said: "neither know we what to do: but our eyes are upon Thee." 2 Chronicles 20:2, 1, 3, 4, 12.

Then upon Jahaziel a Levite "came the Spirit of the Lord; . . . and he said, Hearken ye, all Judah, and ye inhabitants of Jerusalem, and thou King Jehoshaphat, Thus saith the Lord unto you, Be not afraid nor dismayed by reason of this great multitude; for the battle is not yours, but God's. . . . Ye shall not need to fight in this battle: set yourselves, stand ye still, and see the salvation of the Lord. . . . Fear not, nor be dismayed; tomorrow go out against them: for the Lord will be with you." 2 Chronicles 20:14-17.

"And they rose early in the morning, and went forth into the wilderness of Tekoa." 2 Chronicles 20:20. Before the army went singers, lifting their voices in praise to God—praising Him for the victory promised.

On the fourth day thereafter, the army returned to Jerusalem, laden with the spoil of their enemies, singing praise for the victory won.

Through song, David, amidst the vicissitudes of his changeful life, held communion with heaven. How sweetly are his experiences as a shepherd lad reflected in the words:

> "The Lord is my Shepherd; I shall not want.
> He maketh me to lie down in green pastures:
> He leadeth me beside the still waters. . . .
> Though I walk through the valley of the shadow of death,
> I will fear no evil: for Thou art with me;
> Thy rod and Thy staff they comfort me."
>
> Psalm 23:1-4.

In his manhood a hunted fugitive, finding refuge in the rocks and caves of the wilderness, he wrote:

> "O God, Thou art my God; early will I seek Thee:
> My soul thirsteth for Thee, my flesh longeth for Thee,
> In a dry and weary land, where no water is. . . .
> Thou hast been my help,
> And in the shadow of Thy wings will I rejoice."

> "Why art thou cast down, O my soul?
> And why art thou disquieted within me?

Hope thou in God:
For I shall yet praise Him,
Who is the health of my countenance,
And my God."
"The Lord is my light and my salvation;
Whom shall I fear?
The Lord is the strength of my life;
Of whom shall I be afraid?"
Psalms 63:1-7, R.V.; 42:11; 27:1.

The same trust is breathed in the words written when, a dethroned and crownless king, David fled from Jerusalem at the rebellion of Absalom. Spent with grief and the weariness of his flight, he with his company had tarried beside the Jordan for a few hours' rest. He was awakened by the summons to immediate flight. In the darkness, the passage of the deep and swift-flowing stream must be made by that whole company of men, women, and little children; for hard after them were the forces of the traitor son.

In that hour of darkest trial, David sang:

"I cried unto the Lord with my voice,
And He heard me out of His holy hill.

"I laid me down and slept;
I awaked; for the Lord sustained me.
I will not be afraid of ten thousands of people,
That have set themselves against me around about."
Psalm 3:4-6.

After his great sin, in the anguish of remorse and self-abhorrence he still turned to God as his best friend:

"Have mercy upon me, O God, according to Thy loving-kindness:
According unto the multitude of Thy tender mercies blot out
my transgressions. . . .
Purge me with hyssop, and I shall be clean:
Wash me, and I shall be whiter than snow."
Psalm 51:1-7.

In his long Life, David found on earth no resting place. "We are strangers before Thee, and sojourners," he said, "as all our fathers were: our days on the earth are as a shadow, and there is no abiding." I Chronicles 29:15, R.V.

"God is our refuge and strength,
A very present help in trouble.
Therefore will not we fear, though the earth be removed,
And though the mountains be carried into the midst of the sea."
"There is a river, the streams whereof make glad the City of God,
The holy place of the tabernacles of the Most High.
God is in the midst of her; she shall not be moved
God shall help her, at the dawn of morning. . . .
The Lord of hosts is with us;
The God of Jacob is our refuge."

"This God is our God for ever and ever:
He will be our guide even unto death."
Psalms 46:1,2; 46:4-7, R.V., margin; 48:14.

With a song, Jesus in His earthly life met temptation. Often when sharp, stinging words were spoken, often when the atmosphere about Him was heavy with gloom, with dissatisfaction, distrust, or oppressive fear, was heard His song of faith and holy cheer.

On that last sad night of the Passover supper, as He was about to go forth to betrayal and to death, His voice was lifted in the psalm:

"Blessed be the name of the Lord
From this time forth and for evermore.
From the rising of the sun until the going down of the same
The Lord's name is to be praised."

"I love the Lord because He hath heard my voice and my supplications.
Because He hath inclined His ear unto me,
Therefore will I call upon Him as long as I live.

"The sorrows of death compassed me,
And the pains of hell gat hold upon me:
I found trouble and sorrow.
Then called I upon the name of the Lord;
O Lord, I beseech Thee, deliver my soul.
Gracious is the Lord, and righteous;
Yea, our God is merciful.

"The Lord preserveth the simple:
I was brought low, and He helped me.
Return unto thy rest, O my soul;
For the Lord hath dealt bountifully with thee.
For Thou hast delivered my soul from death, mine eyes
from tears, and my feet from falling."
Psalms 113:2, 3; 116:1-8.

Amidst the deepening shadows of earth's last great crisis, God's light will shine brightest, and the song of hope and trust will be heard in clearest and loftiest strains.

"In that day shall this song be sung in the land of Judah;
We have a strong city;
Salvation will God appoint for walls and bulwarks.
Open ye the gates,
That the righteous nation which keepeth the truth may enter in.
Thou wilt keep him in perfect peace,
Whose mind is stayed on Thee: because he trusteth in Thee.
Trust ye in the Lord forever:
For in the Lord Jehovah is everlasting strength."
Isaiah 26:1-4.

"The ransomed of the Lord shall return, and come with singing unto Zion; and everlasting joy shall be upon their heads: they shall obtain gladness and joy, and sorrow and sighing shall flee away." Isaiah 35:10, R.V.

"They shall come and sing in the height of Zion, and shall flow together unto the goodness of the Lord: . . . and their soul shall be as a watered garden; and they shall not sorrow any more at all." Jeremiah 31:12.

The Power of Song

The history of the songs of the Bible is full of suggestion as to the uses and benefits of music and song. Music is often perverted to serve purposes of evil, and it thus becomes one of the most alluring agencies of temptation. But, rightly employed, it is a precious gift of God, designed to uplift the thoughts to high and noble themes, to inspire and elevate the soul.

As the children of Israel, journeying through the wilderness, cheered their way by the music of sacred song, so God bids His children today gladden their pilgrim life. There are few means more effective for fixing His words in the memory than repeating them in song. And such song has wonderful power. It has power to subdue rude and uncultivated natures; power to quicken thought and to awaken sympathy, to promote harmony of action, and to banish the gloom and foreboding that destroy courage and weaken effort.

It is one of the most effective means of impressing the heart with spiritual truth. How often to the soul hard-pressed and ready to despair, memory recalls some word of God's—the long-forgotten burden of a childhood song—and temptations lose their power, life takes on new meaning and new purpose, and courage and gladness are imparted to other souls!

The value of song as a means of education should never be lost sight of. Let there be singing in the home, of songs that are sweet and pure, and there will be fewer words of censure and more of cheerfulness and hope and joy. Let there be singing in the school, and the pupils will be drawn closer to God, to their teachers, and to one another.

As a part of religious service, singing is as much an act of worship as is prayer. Indeed, many a song is prayer. If the child is taught to realize this, he will think more of the meaning of the words he sings and will be more susceptible to their power.

As our Redeemer leads us to the threshold of the Infinite, flushed with the glory of God, we may catch the themes of praise and thanksgiving from the heavenly choir round about the throne; and as the echo of the angels' song is awakened in our earthly homes, hearts will be drawn closer to the heavenly singers. Heaven's communion begins on earth. We learn here the keynote of its praise.

18
Mysteries of the Bible

"Canst thou by searching find out God?"

No finite mind can fully comprehend the character or the works of the Infinite One. We cannot by searching find out God. To minds the strongest and most highly cultured, as well as to the weakest and most ignorant, that holy Being must remain clothed in mystery. But though "clouds and darkness are round about Him: righteousness and judgment are the foundation of His throne." Psalm 97:2, R.V. We can so far comprehend His dealing with us as to discern boundless mercy united to infinite power. We can understand as much of His purposes as we are capable of comprehending; beyond this we may still trust the hand that is omnipotent, the heart that is full of love.

The word of God, like the character of its Author, presents mysteries that can never be fully comprehended by finite beings. But God has given in the Scriptures sufficient evidence of their divine authority. His own existence, His character, the truthfulness of His word, are established by testimony that appeals to our reason; and this testimony is abundant. True, He has not removed the possibility of doubt; faith must rest upon evidence, not demonstration; those who wish to doubt have opportunity; but those who desire to know the truth find ample ground for faith.

We have no reason to doubt God's word because we cannot understand the mysteries of His providence. In the natural world we are constantly surrounded with wonders beyond our comprehension. Should we then be surprised to find in the spiritual world also mysteries that we cannot fathom? The difficulty lies solely in the weakness and narrowness of the human mind.

The mysteries of the Bible, so far from being an argument against it, are among the strongest evidences of its divine inspiration. If it contained no account of God but that which we could comprehend; if His greatness and majesty could be grasped by finite minds, then the Bible would not, as now, bear the unmistakable evidences of divinity. The greatness of its themes should inspire faith in it as the word of God.

The Bible unfolds truth with a simplicity and an adaptation to the needs and longings of the human heart that has astonished and charmed the most highly cultivated minds, while to the humble and uncultured also it makes plain the way of life. "The wayfaring men, though fools, shall not err therein," Isaiah 35:8. No child need mistake the path. Not one trembling seeker need fail of walking in pure and holy light. Yet the most simply stated truths lay hold upon themes elevated, far-reaching, infinitely beyond the power of human comprehension—mysteries that are the hiding of His glory, mysteries that overpower the mind in its research—while they inspire the sincere seeker for truth with reverence and faith. The more we search the Bible, the deeper is our conviction that it is the word of the living God, and human reason bows before the majesty of divine revelation.

God intends that to the earnest seeker the truths of His word shall be ever unfolding. While "the secret things belong unto the Lord our God," "those things which are revealed belong unto us and to our children." Deuteronomy 29:29. The idea that certain portions of the Bible cannot be understood has led to neglect of some of its most important truths. The fact needs to be emphasized, and often repeated, that the mysteries of the Bible are not such because God has sought to conceal truth, but because our own weakness or ignorance makes us incapable of comprehending or appropriating truth. The limitation is not in His purpose, but in our capacity. Of those very portions of Scripture often passed by as impossible to be understood, God desires us to understand as much as our minds are capable of receiving. "All Scripture is given by inspiration of God," that we may be "throughly furnished unto all good works," 2 Timothy 3:16, 17.

It is impossible for any human mind to exhaust even one truth or promise of the Bible. One catches the glory from one point of view, another from another point; yet we can discern only gleamings. The full radiance is beyond our vision.

As we contemplate the great things of God's word, we look into a fountain that broadens and deepens beneath our gaze. Its breadth and depth pass our knowledge. As we gaze, the vision widens; stretched out before us we behold a boundless, shoreless sea.

Such study has vivifying power. The mind and heart acquire new strength, new life.

This experience is the highest evidence of the divine authorship of the Bible. We receive God's word as food for the soul, through the same evidence by which we receive bread as food for the body. Bread supplies the need of our nature; we know by experience that it produces blood and bone and brain. Apply the same test to the Bible; when its principles have actually become the elements of character, what has been the result? what changes have been made in the life? "Old things are passed away; behold, all things are become new." 2 Corinthians 5:17. In its power, men and women have broken the chains of sinful habit. They have renounced selfishness. The profane have become reverent, the drunken sober, the profligate pure. Souls that have borne the likeness of Satan have been transformed into the image of God. This change is itself the miracle of miracles. A change wrought by the word, it is one of the deepest mysteries of the word. We cannot understand it;

we can only believe, as declared by the Scriptures, it is "Christ in you, the hope of glory." Colossians 1:27.

A knowledge of this mystery furnishes a key to every other. It opens to the soul the treasures of the universe, the possibilities of infinite development.

And this development is gained through the constant unfolding to us of the character of God—the glory and the mystery of the written word. If it were possible for us to attain to a full understanding of God and His word, there would be for us no further discovery of truth, no greater knowledge, no further development. God would cease to be supreme, and man would cease to advance. Thank God, it is not so. Since God is infinite, and in Him are all the treasures of wisdom, we may to all eternity be ever searching, ever learning, yet never exhaust the riches of His wisdom, His goodness, or His power.

19
History and Prophecy

"Who hath declared this from ancient time? . . . Have not I the Lord? And there is no god else."

The Bible is the most ancient and the most comprehensive history that men possess. It came fresh from the fountain of eternal truth, and throughout the ages a divine hand has preserved its purity. It lights up the far-distant past, where human research in vain seeks to penetrate. In God's word only do we behold the power that laid the foundations of the earth and that stretched out the heavens. Here only do we find an authentic account of the origin of nations. Here only is given a history of our race unsullied by human pride or prejudice.

In the annals of human history the growth of nations, the rise and fall of empires, appear as dependent on the will and prowess of man. The shaping of events seems, to a great degree, to be determined by his power, ambition, or caprice. But in the word of God the curtain is drawn aside, and we behold, behind, above, and through all the play and counterplay of human interests and power and passions, the agencies of the all-merciful One, silently, patiently working out the counsels of His own will.

The Bible reveals the true philosophy of history. In those words of matchless beauty and tenderness spoken by the apostle Paul to the sages of Athens is set forth God's purpose in the creation and distribution of races and nations: He "hath made of one blood all nations of men for to dwell on all the face of the earth, and hath determined the times before appointed, and the bounds of their habitation; that they should seek the Lord, if haply they might feel after Him, and find Him." Acts 17:26, 27. God declares that whosoever will may come "into the bond of the covenant." Ezekiel 20:37. In the creation it was His purpose that the earth be inhabited by beings whose existence should be a blessing to themselves and to one another, and an honor to their Creator. All who will may identify themselves with this purpose. Of them it is spoken, "This people have I formed for Myself; they shall show forth My praise." Isaiah 43:21.

God has revealed in His law the principles that underlie all true prosperity both of nations and of individuals. "This is your wisdom and your understanding," Moses declared to the Israelites of the law of God. "It is not a vain thing for you; because it is your life." Deuteronomy 4:6; 32:47. The blessings thus assured to Israel are, on the same conditions and in the same degree, assured to every nation and every individual under the broad heavens.

The power exercised by every ruler on the earth is Heaven-imparted; and upon his use of the power thus bestowed, his success depends. To each the word of the divine Watcher is, "I girded thee, though thou hast not known Me." Isaiah 45:5. And to each the words spoken to Nebuchadnezzar of old are the lesson of life: "Break off thy sins by righteousness, and thine iniquities by showing mercy to the poor; if it may be a lengthening of thy tranquility." Daniel 4:27.

To understand these things—to understand that "righteousness exalteth a nation;" that "the throne is established by righteousness" and "upholden by mercy" (Proverbs 14:34; 16:12; 20:28); to recognize the outworking of these principles in the manifestation of His power who "removeth kings, and setteth up kings" (Daniel 2:21)—this is to understand the philosophy of history.

In the word of God only is this clearly set forth. Here it is shown that the strength of nations, as of individuals, is not found in the opportunities or facilities that appear to make them invincible; it is not found in their boasted greatness. It is measured by the fidelity with which they fulfill God's purpose.

An illustration of this truth is found in the history of ancient Babylon. To Nebuchadnezzar the king the true object of national government was represented under the figure of a great tree, whose height "reached unto heaven, and the sight thereof to the end of all the earth: the leaves thereof were fair, and the fruit thereof much, and in it was meat for all;" under its shadow the beasts of the field dwelt, and among its branches the birds of the air had their habitation. Daniel 4:11, 12. This representation shows the character of a government that fulfills God's purpose—a government that protects and upbuilds the nation.

God exalted Babylon that it might fulfill this purpose. Prosperity attended the nation until it reached a height of wealth and power that has never since been equaled—fitly represented in the Scriptures by the inspired symbol, a "head of gold." Daniel 2:38.

But the king failed of recognizing the power that had exalted him. Nebuchadnezzar in the pride of his heart said: "Is not this great Babylon, that I have built for the house of the kingdom by the might of my power, and for the honor of my majesty?" Daniel 4:30.

Instead of being a protector of men, Babylon became a proud and cruel oppressor. The words of Inspiration picturing the cruelty and greed of rulers in Israel reveal the secret of Babylon's fall and of the fall of many another kingdom since the world began: "Ye eat the fat, and ye clothe you with the wool, ye kill them that are fed: but ye feed not the flock. The diseased have ye not strengthened, neither have ye healed that which was sick, neither have ye bound up that which was broken, neither have ye brought again that which was driven away, neither have ye sought that which was lost; but with force and with cruelty have ye ruled them." Ezekiel 34:3, 4.

To the ruler of Babylon came the sentence of the divine Watcher: O king, "to thee it is spoken; The kingdom is departed from thee." Daniel 4:31.

"Come down, and sit in the dust, O virgin daughter of Babylon,
Sit on the ground: there is no throne. . . .
Sit thou silent,
And get thee into darkness, O daughter of the Chaldeans;
For thou shalt no more be called, The lady of kingdoms."
Isaiah 47:1-5.

"O thou that dwellest upon many waters, abundant in treasures,
Thine end is come, and the measure of thy covetousness,"
"Babylon, the glory of kingdoms,
The beauty of the Chaldees' excellency,
Shall be as when God overthrew Sodom and Gomorrah."

"I will also make it a possession for the bittern, and pools of water: and I will sweep it with the besom of destruction, saith the Lord of hosts." Jeremiah 51:13; Isaiah 13:19; 14:23.

Every nation that has come upon the stage of action has been permitted to occupy its place on the earth, that it might be seen whether it would fulfill the purpose of "the Watcher and the Holy One." Prophecy has traced the rise and fall of the world's great empires—Babylon, Medo-Persia, Greece, and Rome. With each of these, as with nations of less power, history repeated itself. Each had its period of test, each failed, its glory faded, its power departed, and its place was occupied by another.

While the nations rejected God's principles, and in this rejection wrought their own ruin, it was still manifest that the divine, overruling purpose was working through all their movements.

This lesson is taught in a wonderful symbolic representation given to the prophet Ezekiel during his exile in the land of the Chaldeans. The vision was given at a time when Ezekiel was weighed down with sorrowful memories and troubled forebodings. The land of his fathers was desolate. Jerusalem was depopulated. The prophet himself was a stranger in a land where ambition and cruelty reigned supreme. As on every hand he beheld tyranny and wrong, his soul was distressed, and he mourned day and night. But the symbols presented to him revealed a power above that of earthly rulers.

Upon the banks of the river Chebar, Ezekiel beheld a whirlwind seeming to come from the north, "a great cloud, and a fire infolding itself, and a brightness was about it, and out of the midst thereof as the color of amber." A number of wheels, intersecting one another, were moved by four living beings. High above all these "was the likeness of a throne, as the appearance of a sapphire stone: and upon the likeness of the throne was the likeness as the appearance of a man above upon it." "And there appeared in the cherubims the form of a man's hand under their wings." Ezekiel 1:4, 26, 10:8. The wheels were so complicated in arrangement that at first sight they appeared to be in confusion; but they moved in perfect harmony. Heavenly beings, sustained and guided by the hand beneath the wings of the cherubim, were impelling these wheels; above them, upon the sapphire throne, was the Eternal One; and round about the throne a rainbow, the emblem of divine mercy.

As the wheellike complications were under the guidance of the hand beneath the wings of the cherubim, so the complicated play of human events is under divine control. Amidst the strife and tumult of nations, He that sitteth above the cherubim still guides the affairs of the earth.

The history of nations that one after another have occupied their allotted time and place, unconsciously witnessing to the truth of which they themselves knew not the meaning, speaks to us. To every nation and to every individual of today God has assigned a place in His great plan. Today men and nations are being measured by the plummet in the hand of Him who makes no mistake. All are by their own choice deciding their destiny, and God is overruling all for the accomplishment of His purposes.

The history which the great I AM has marked out in His word, uniting link after link in the prophetic chain, from eternity in the past to eternity in the future, tells us where we are today in the procession of the ages, and what may be expected in the time to come. All that prophecy has foretold as coming to pass, until the present time, has been traced on the pages of history, and we may be assured that all which is yet to come will be fulfilled in its order.

The final overthrow of all earthly dominions is plainly foretold in the word of truth. In the prophecy uttered when sentence from God was pronounced upon the last king of Israel is given the message:

"Thus saith the Lord God; Remove the diadem, and take off the crown: . . . exalt him that is low, and abase him that is high. I will overturn, overturn, overturn, it: and it shall be no more, until He come whose right it is; and I will give it Him." Ezekiel 21:26, 27.

The crown removed from Israel passed successively to the kingdoms of Babylon, Medo-Persia, Greece, and Rome. God says, "It shall be no more, until He come whose right it is; and I will give it Him."

That time is at hand. Today the signs of the times declare that we are standing on the threshold of great and solemn events. Everything in our world is in agitation. Before our eyes is fulfilling the Saviour's prophecy of the events to precede His coming: "Ye shall hear of wars and rumors of wars. . . . Nation shall rise against nation, and kingdom against kingdom: and there shall be famines, and pestilences, and earthquakes, in divers places." Matthew 24:6, 7.

The present is a time of overwhelming interest to all living. Rulers and statesmen, men who occupy positions of trust and authority, thinking men and women of all classes, have their attention fixed upon the events taking place about us. They are watching the strained, restless relations that exist among the nations. They observe the intensity that is taking possession of every earthly element, and they recognize that something great and decisive is about to take place—that the world is on the verge of a stupendous crisis.

Angels are now restraining the winds of strife, that they may not blow until the world shall be warned of its coming doom; but a storm is gathering, ready to burst upon the earth; and when God shall bid His angels loose the winds, there will be such a scene of strife as no pen can picture.

The Bible, and the Bible only, gives a correct view of these things. Here are revealed the great final scenes in the history of our world, events that already are casting their shadows before, the sound of their approach causing the earth to tremble and men's hearts to fail them for fear.

"Behold, the Lord maketh the earth empty, and maketh it waste, and turneth it upside down, and scattereth abroad the inhabitants thereof. . . . They have transgressed the laws, changed the ordinance, broken the everlasting covenant. Therefore hath the curse devoured the earth, and they that dwell therein are desolate. . . . The mirth of tabrets ceaseth, the noise of them that rejoice endeth, the joy of the harp ceaseth." Isaiah 24:1-8.

"Alas for the day! for the day of the Lord is at hand, and as a destruction from the Almighty shall it come. . . . The seed is rotten under their clods, the garners are laid desolate, the barns are broken down; for the corn is withered. How do the beasts groan! the herds of cattle are perplexed, because they have no pasture; yea, the flocks of sheep are made desolate." "The vine is dried up, and the fig tree languisheth; the pomegranate tree, the palm tree also, and the apple tree, even all the trees of the field, are withered: because joy is withered away from the sons of men." Joel 1:15-18, 12.

"I am pained at my very heart; . . . I cannot hold my peace, because thou hast heard, O my soul, the sound of the trumpet, the alarm of war. Destruction upon destruction is cried; for the whole land is spoiled."

"I beheld the earth, and, lo, it was without form, and void; and the heavens, and they had no light. I beheld the mountains, and, lo, they trembled, and all the hills moved lightly. I beheld, and, lo, there was no man, and all the birds of the heavens were fled. I beheld, and, lo, the fruitful place was a wilderness, and all the cities thereof were broken down." Jeremiah 4:19, 20, 23-26.

"Alas! for that day is great, so that none is like it: it is even the time of Jacob's trouble; but he shall be saved out of it." Jeremiah 30:7.

"Come, My people, enter thou into thy chambers, and shut thy doors about thee: hide thyself as it were for a little moment, until the indignation be overpast." Isaiah 26:20.

> "Because thou hast made the Lord, which is my refuge,
> Even the Most High, thy habitation;
> There shall no evil befall thee,
> Neither shall any plague come nigh thy dwelling."
> Psalm 91:9, 10.

"The mighty God, even the Lord, hath spoken,
And called the earth from the rising of the sun unto the going down thereof.
Out of Zion, the perfection of beauty, God hath shined.
Our God shall come, and shall not keep silence."

"He shall call to the heavens above,
And to the earth, that He may judge His people. . . .
And the heavens shall declare His righteousness;
For God is judge Himself."

Psalm 50:1-3; 50:4-6, R.V.

"O daughter of Zion, . . . the Lord shall redeem thee from the hand of thine enemies. Now also many nations are gathered against thee, that say, Let her be defiled, and let our eye look upon Zion. But they know not the thoughts of the Lord, neither understand they His counsel." "Because they call thee an Outcast, saying, This is Zion, whom no man seeketh after," "I will restore health unto thee, and I will heal thee of thy wounds, saith the Lord." "I will bring again the captivity of Jacob's tents, and have mercy on his dwelling places." Micah 4:10-12; Jeremiah 30:17, 18.

"And it shall be said in that day, Lo, this is our God;
We have waited for Him, and He will save us:
This is the Lord; we have waited for Him,
We will be glad and rejoice in His salvation."

"He will swallow up death in victory; . . . and the rebuke of His people shall He take away from off all the earth: for the Lord hath spoken it." Isaiah 25:9, 8.

"Look upon Zion, the city of our solemnities: thine eyes shall see Jerusalem a quiet habitation, a tabernacle that shall not be taken down. . . . For the Lord is our judge, the Lord is our lawgiver, the Lord is our king." Isaiah 33:20-22.

"With righteousness shall He judge the poor, and reprove with equity for the meek of the earth." Isaiah 11:4.

Then will the purpose of God be fulfilled; the principles of His kingdom will be honored by all beneath the sun.

"Violence shall no more be heard in thy land,
Wasting nor destruction within thy borders;
But thou shalt call thy walls Salvation,
And thy gates Praise."

"In righteousness shalt thou be established:
Thou shalt be far from oppression; for thou shalt not fear:
And from terror; for it shall not come near thee."

Isaiah 60:18; 54:14.

The prophets to whom these great scenes were revealed longed to understand their import. They "inquired and searched diligently: . . . searching what, or what manner of time the Spirit of Christ which was in them did signify. . . . Unto whom it was revealed, that not unto themselves, but unto us they did minister the things, which are now reported unto you; . . . which things the angels desire to look into." 1 Peter 1:10-12.

To us who are standing on the very verge of their fulfillment, of what deep moment, what living interest, are these delineations of the things to come—events for which, since our first parents turned their steps from Eden, God's children have watched and waited, longed and prayed!

At this time, before the great final crisis, as before the world's first destruction, men are absorbed in the pleasures and the pursuits of sense. Engrossed with the seen and transitory, they have lost sight of the unseen and eternal. For the things that perish with the using, they are sacrificing imperishable riches. Their minds need to be uplifted, their views of life to be broadened. They need to be aroused from the lethargy of worldly dreaming.

From the rise and fall of nations as made plain in the pages of Holy Writ, they need to learn how worthless is mere outward and worldly glory. Babylon, with all its power and its magnificence, the like of which our world has never since beheld—power and magnificence which to the people of that day seemed so stable and enduring—how completely has it passed away! As "the flower of the grass" it has perished. So perishes all that has not God for its foundation. Only that which is bound up with His purpose and expresses His character can endure. His principles are the only steadfast things our world knows.

It is these great truths that old and young need to learn. We need to study the working out of God's purpose in the history of nations and in the revelation of things to come, that we may estimate at their true value things seen and things unseen; that we may learn what is the true aim of life; that, viewing the things of time in the light of eternity, we may put them to their truest and noblest use. Thus, learning here the principles of His kingdom and becoming its subjects and citizens, we may be prepared at His coming to enter with Him into its possession.

The day is at hand. For the lessons to be learned, the work to be done, the transformation of character to be effected, the time remaining is but too brief a span.

"Behold, they of the house of Israel say, The vision that he seeth is for many days to come, and he prophesieth of the times that are far off. Therefore say unto them, Thus saith the Lord God; There shall none of My words be prolonged any more, but the word which I have spoken shall be done, saith the Lord God." Ezekiel 12:27, 28.

20
Bible Teaching and Study

"Incline thine ear unto wisdom." "Search for her as for hid treasures."

In childhood, youth, and manhood, Jesus studied the Scriptures. As a little child He was daily at His mother's knee taught from the scrolls of the prophets. In His youth the early morning and the evening twilight often found Him alone on the mountainside or among the trees of the forest, spending a quiet hour in prayer and the study of God's word. During His ministry His intimate acquaintance with the Scriptures testifies to His diligence in their study. And since He gained knowledge as we may gain it, His wonderful power, both mental and spiritual, is a testimony to the value of the Bible as a means of education.

Our heavenly Father, in giving His word, did not overlook the children. In all that men have written, where can be found anything that has such a hold upon the heart, anything so well adapted to awaken the interest of the little ones, as the stories of the Bible?

In these simple stories may be made plain the great principles of the law of God. Thus by illustrations best suited to the child's comprehension, parents and teachers may begin very early to fulfill the Lord's injunction concerning His precepts: "Thou shalt teach them diligently unto thy children, and shalt talk of them when thou sittest in thine house, and when thou walkest by the way, and when thou liest down, and when thou risest up." Deuteronomy 6:7.

The use of object lessons, blackboards, maps, and pictures, will be an aid in explaining these lessons, and fixing them in the memory. Parents and teachers should constantly seek for improved methods. The teaching of the Bible should have our freshest thought, our best methods, and our most earnest effort.

In arousing and strengthening a love for Bible study, much depends on the use of the hour of worship. The hours of morning and evening worship should be the sweetest and most helpful of the day. Let it be understood that into these hours no troubled, unkind thoughts are to intrude; that parents and children assemble to meet with Jesus, and to invite into the home the presence of holy angels. Let the services be brief and full of life, adapted to the occasion, and varied from time to time. Let all join in the Bible reading and learn and often repeat God's law. It will add to the interest of the children if they are sometimes permitted to select the reading. Question them upon it, and let them ask questions. Mention anything that will serve to illustrate its meaning. When the service is not thus made too lengthy, let the little ones take part in prayer, and let them join in song, if it be but a single verse.

To make such a service what it should be, thought should be given to preparation. And parents should take time daily for Bible study with their children. No doubt it will require effort and planning and some sacrifice to accomplish this; but the effort will be richly repaid.

As a preparation for teaching His precepts, God commands that they be hidden in the hearts of the parents. "These words, which I command thee this day, shall be in thine heart," He says; "and thou shalt teach them diligently." Deuteronomy 6:6, 7. In order to interest our children in the Bible, we ourselves must be interested in it. To awaken in them a love for its study, we must love it. Our instruction to them will have only the weight of influence given it by our own example and spirit.

God called Abraham to be a teacher of His word, He chose him to be the father of a great nation, because He saw that Abraham would instruct his children and his household in the principles of God's law. And that which gave power to Abraham's teaching was the influence of his own life. His great household consisted of more than a thousand souls, many of them heads of families, and not a few but newly converted from heathenism. Such a household required a firm hand at the helm. No weak, vacillating methods would suffice. Of Abraham God said, "I know him, that he will command his children and his household after him." Genesis 18:19. Yet his authority was exercised with such wisdom and tenderness that hearts were won. The testimony of the divine Watcher is, "They shall keep the way of the Lord, to do justice and judgment." Genesis 18:19. And Abraham's influence extended beyond his own household. Wherever he pitched his tent, he set up beside it the altar for sacrifice and worship. When the tent was removed, the altar remained; and many a roving Canaanite, whose knowledge of God had been gained from the life of Abraham His servant, tarried at that altar to offer sacrifice to Jehovah.

No less effective today will be the teaching of God's word when it finds as faithful a reflection in the teacher's life.

It is not enough to know what others have thought or learned about the Bible. Everyone must in the judgment give account of himself to God, and each should now learn for himself what is truth. But in order to do effective study, the interest of the pupil must be enlisted. Especially by the one who has to deal with children and youth differing widely in disposition, training, and habits of thought, this is a matter not to be lost sight of. In teaching children the Bible, we may gain much by observing the bent of their minds, the things in which they are interested, and arousing their interest to see what the Bible says about these things. He who created us, with our various aptitudes, has in His word given something for everyone. As the pupils see that the lessons of the Bible apply to their own lives, teach them to look to it as a counselor.

Help them also to appreciate its wonderful beauty. Many books of no real value, books that are exciting and unhealthful are recommended, or at least permitted to be used, because of their supposed literary value. Why should we direct our children to drink of these polluted streams when they may have free access to the pure fountains of the word of God? The Bible has a fullness, a strength, a depth of meaning, that is inexhaustible. Encourage the children and youth to seek out its treasures both of thought and of expression.

As the beauty of these precious things attracts their minds, a softening, subduing power will touch their hearts. They will be drawn to Him who has thus revealed Himself to them. And there are few who will not desire to know more of His works and ways.

The student of the Bible should be taught to approach it in the spirit of a learner. We are to search its pages, not for proof to sustain our opinions, but in order to know what God says.

A true knowledge of the Bible can be gained only through the aid of that Spirit by whom the word was given. And in order to gain this knowledge we must live by it. All that God's word commands, we are to obey. All that it promises, we may claim. The life which it enjoins is the life that, through its power, we are to live. Only as the Bible is thus held can it be studied effectively.

The study of the Bible demands our most diligent effort and persevering thought. As the miner digs for the golden treasure in the earth, so earnestly, persistently, must we seek for the treasure of God's word.

In daily study the verse-by-verse method is often most helpful. Let the student take one verse, and concentrate the mind on ascertaining the thought that God has put into that verse for him, and then dwell upon the thought until it becomes his own. One passage thus studied until its significance is clear is of more value than the perusal of many chapters with no definite purpose in view and no positive instruction gained.

One of the chief causes of mental inefficiency and moral weakness is the lack of concentration for worthy ends. We pride ourselves on the wide distribution of literature; but the multiplication of books, even books that in themselves are not harmful, may be a positive evil. With the immense tide of printed matter constantly pouring from the press, old and young form the habit of reading hastily and superficially, and the mind loses its power of connected and vigorous thought. Furthermore, a large share of the periodicals and books that, like the frogs of Egypt, are overspreading the land, are not merely commonplace, idle, and enervating, but unclean and degrading. Their effect is not merely to intoxicate and ruin the mind, but to corrupt and destroy the soul. The mind, the heart, that is indolent, aimless, falls an easy prey to evil. It is on diseased, lifeless organisms that fungus roots. It is the idle mind that is Satan's workshop. Let the mind be directed to high and holy ideals, let the life have a noble aim, an absorbing purpose, and evil finds little foothold.

Let the youth, then, be taught to give close study to the word of God. Received into the soul, it will prove a mighty barricade against temptation. "Thy word," the psalmist declares, "have I hid in mine heart, that I might not sin against Thee." "By the word of Thy lips I have kept me from the paths of the destroyer." Psalms 119:11; 17:4.

The Bible is its own expositor. Scripture is to be compared with scripture. The student should learn to view the word as a whole, and to see the relation of its parts. He should gain a knowledge of its grand central theme, of God's original purpose for the world, of the rise of the great controversy, and of the work of redemption. He should understand the nature of the two principles that are contending for supremacy, and should learn to trace their working through the records of history and prophecy, to the great consummation. He should see how this controversy enters into every phase of human experience; how in every act of life he himself reveals the one or the other of the two antagonistic motives; and how, whether he will or not, he is even now deciding upon which side of the controversy he will be found.

Every part of the Bible is given by inspiration of God and is profitable. The Old Testament no less than the New should receive attention. As we study the Old Testament we shall find living springs bubbling up where the careless reader discerns only a desert.

The book of Revelation, in connection with the book of Daniel, especially demands study. Let every God-fearing teacher consider how most clearly to comprehend and to present the gospel that our Saviour came in person to make known to His servant John—"The Revelation of Jesus Christ, which God gave unto Him, to show unto His servants things which must shortly come to pass." Revelation 1:1. None should become discouraged in the study of the Revelation because of its apparently mystical symbols. "If any of you lack wisdom, let him ask of God, that giveth to all men liberally, and upbraideth not." James 1:5.

"Blessed is he that readeth, and they that hear the words of this prophecy, and keep those things which are written therein: for the time is at hand." Revelation 1:3.

When a real love for the Bible is awakened, and the student begins to realize how vast is the field and how precious its treasure, he will desire to seize upon every opportunity for acquainting himself with God's word. Its study will be restricted to no special time or place. And this continuous study is one of the best means of cultivating a love for the Scriptures. Let the student keep his Bible always with him. As you have opportunity, read a text and meditate upon it. While walking the streets, waiting at a railway station, waiting to meet an engagement, improve the opportunity to gain some precious thought from the treasure house of truth.

The great motive powers of the soul are faith, hope, and love; and it is to these that Bible study, rightly pursued, appeals. The outward beauty of the Bible, the beauty of imagery and expression, is but the setting, as it were, for its real treasure—the beauty of holiness. In its record of the men who walked with God, we may catch glimpses of His glory. In the One "altogether lovely" we behold Him, of whom all beauty of earth and heaven is but a dim reflection. "I, if I be lifted up," He said, "will draw all men unto Me." John 12:32. As the student of the Bible beholds the Redeemer, there is awakened in the soul the mysterious power of faith, adoration, and love. Upon the vision of Christ the gaze is fixed, and the beholder grows into the likeness of that which he adores. The words of the apostle Paul become the language of the soul: "I count all things but loss for the excellency of the knowledge of Christ Jesus my Lord: . . . that I may know Him, and the power of His resurrection, and the fellowship of His sufferings." Philippians 3:8-10.

The springs of heavenly peace and joy unsealed in the soul by the words of Inspiration will become a mighty river of influence to bless all who come within its reach. Let the youth of today, the youth who are growing up with the Bible in their hands, become the recipients and the channels of its life-giving energy, and what streams of blessing would flow forth to the world!—influences of whose power to heal and comfort we can scarcely conceive—rivers of living water, fountains "springing up unto everlasting life."

Physical Culture

"Beloved, I wish above all things that thou mayest prosper and be in health, even as thy soul prospereth."

21
Study of Physiology

"I am fearfully and wonderfully made."

Since the mind and the soul find expression through the body, both mental and spiritual vigor are in great degree dependent upon physical strength and activity; whatever promotes physical health, promotes the development of a strong mind and a well-balanced character. Without health no one can as distinctly understand or as completely fulfill his obligations to himself, to his fellow beings, or to his Creator. Therefore the health should be as faithfully guarded as the character. A knowledge of physiology and hygiene should be the basis of all educational effort.

Though the facts of physiology are now so generally understood, there is an alarming indifference in regard to the principles of health. Even of those who have a knowledge of these principles, there are few who put them in practice. Inclination or impulse is followed as blindly as if life were controlled by mere chance rather than by definite and unvarying laws.

The youth, in the freshness and vigor of life, little realize the value of their abounding energy. A treasure more precious than gold, more essential to advancement than learning or rank or riches—how lightly it is held! how rashly squandered! How many a man, sacrificing health in the struggle for riches or power, has almost reached the object of his desire, only to fall helpless, while another, possessing superior physical endurance, grasped the longed-for prize! Through morbid conditions, the result of neglecting the laws of health, how many have been led into evil practices, to the sacrifice of every hope for this world and the next!

In the study of physiology, pupils should be led to see the value of physical energy and how it can be so preserved and developed as to contribute in the highest degree to success in life's great struggle.

Children should be early taught, in simple, easy lessons, the rudiments of physiology and hygiene. The work should be begun by the mother in the home and should be faithfully carried forward in the school. As the pupils advance in years, instruction in this line should be continued until they are qualified to care for the house they live in. They should understand the importance of guarding against disease by preserving the vigor of every organ and should also be taught how to deal with common diseases and accidents. Every school should give instruction in both physiology and hygiene, and, so far as possible, should be provided with facilities for illustrating the structure, use, and care of the body.

There are matters not usually included in the study of physiology that should be considered—matters of far greater value to the student than are many of the technicalities commonly taught under this head. As the foundation principle of all education in these lines, the youth should be taught that the laws of nature are the laws of God—as truly divine as are the precepts of the Decalogue. The laws that govern our physical organism, God has written upon every nerve, muscle, and fiber of the body. Every careless or willful violation of these laws is a sin against our Creator.

How necessary, then, that a thorough knowledge of these laws should be imparted! The principles of hygiene as applied to diet, exercise, the care of children, the treatment of the sick, and many like matters, should be given much more attention than they ordinarily receive.

The influence of the mind on the body, as well as of the body on the mind, should be emphasized. The electric power of the brain, promoted by mental activity, vitalizes the whole system, and is thus an invaluable aid in resisting disease. This should be made plain. The power of the will and the importance of self-control, both in the preservation and in the recovery of health, the depressing and even ruinous effect of anger, discontent, selfishness, or impurity, and, on the other hand, the marvelous life-giving power to be found in cheerfulness, unselfishness, gratitude, should also be shown.

There is a physiological truth—truth that we need to consider—in the scripture, "A merry [rejoicing] heart doeth good like a medicine." Proverbs 17:22.

"Let thine heart keep My commandments," God says; "for length of days, and years of life, and peace, shall they add to thee." "They are life unto those that find them, and health to all their flesh." "Pleasant words" the Scriptures declare to be not only "sweet to the soul," but "health to the bones." Proverbs 3:1, 2, margin; 4:22; 16:24.

The youth need to understand the deep truth underlying the Bible statement that with God "is the fountain of life." Psalm 36:9. Not only is He the originator of all, but He is the life of everything that lives. It is His life that we receive in the sunshine, in the pure, sweet air, in the food which builds up our bodies and sustains our strength. It is by His life that we exist, hour by hour, moment by moment. Except as perverted by sin, all His gifts tend to life, to health and joy.

"He hath made everything beautiful in its time" (Ecclesiastes 3:11, R.V.); and true beauty will be secured, not in marring God's work, but in coming into harmony with the laws of Him who created all things, and who finds pleasure in their beauty and perfection.

As the mechanism of the body is studied, attention should be directed to its wonderful adaptation of means to ends, the harmonious action and dependence of the various organs. As the interest of the student is thus awakened, and he is led to see the importance of physical culture, much can be done by the teacher to secure proper development and right habits.

Among the first things to be aimed at should be a correct position, both in sitting and in standing. God made man upright, and He desires him to possess not only the physical but the mental and moral benefit, the grace and dignity and self-possession, the courage and self-reliance, which an erect bearing so greatly tends to promote. Let the teacher give instruction on this point by example and by precept. Show what a correct position is, and insist that it shall be maintained.

Next in importance to right position are respiration and vocal culture. The one who sits and stands erect is more likely than others to breathe properly. But the teacher should impress upon his pupils the importance of deep breathing. Show how the healthy action of the respiratory organs, assisting the circulation of the blood, invigorates the whole system, excites the appetite, promotes digestion, and induces sound, sweet sleep, thus not only refreshing the body, but soothing and tranquilizing the mind. And while the importance of deep breathing is shown, the practice should be insisted upon. Let exercises be given which will promote this, and see that the habit becomes established.

The training of the voice has an important place in physical culture, since it tends to expand and strengthen the lungs, and thus to ward off disease. To ensure correct delivery in reading and speaking, see that the abdominal muscles have full play in breathing and that the respiratory organs are unrestricted. Let the strain come on the muscles of the abdomen rather than on those of the throat. Great weariness and serious disease of the throat and lungs may thus be prevented. Careful attention should be given to securing distinct articulation, smooth, well-modulated tones, and a not-too-rapid delivery. This will not only promote health, but will add greatly to the agreeableness and efficiency of the student's work.

In teaching these things a golden opportunity is afforded for showing the folly and wickedness of tight lacing and every other practice that restricts vital action. An almost endless train of disease results from unhealthful modes of dress, and careful instruction on this point should be given. Impress upon the pupils the danger of allowing the clothing to weigh on the hips or to compress any organ of the body. The dress should be so arranged that a full respiration can be taken and the arms be raised above the head without difficulty. The cramping of the lungs not only prevents their development, but hinders the processes of digestion and circulation, and thus weakens the whole body. All such practices lessen both physical and mental power, thus hindering the student's advancement and often preventing his success.

In the study of hygiene the earnest teacher will improve every opportunity to show the necessity of perfect cleanliness both in personal habits and in all one's surroundings. The value of the daily bath in promoting health and in stimulating mental action, should be emphasized. Attention should be given also to sunlight and ventilation, the hygiene of the sleeping room and the kitchen. Teach the pupils that a healthful sleeping room, a thoroughly clean kitchen, and a tastefully arranged, wholesomely supplied table, will go further toward securing the happiness of the family and the regard of every sensible visitor than any amount of expensive furnishing in the drawing room. That "the life is more than meat, and the body is more than raiment" (Luke 12:23), is a lesson no less needed now than when given by the divine Teacher eighteen hundred years ago.

The student of physiology should be taught that the object of his study is not merely to gain a knowledge of facts and principles. This alone will prove of little benefit. He may understand the importance of ventilation, his room may be supplied with pure air; but unless he fills his lungs properly he will suffer the results of imperfect respiration. So the necessity of cleanliness may be understood, and needful facilities may be supplied; but all will be without avail unless put to use. The great requisite in teaching these principles is to impress the pupil with their importance so that he will conscientiously put them in practice.

By a most beautiful and impressive figure, God's word shows the regard He places upon our physical organism and the responsibility resting on us to preserve it in the best condition: "Know ye not that your body is a temple of the Holy Spirit which is in you, which ye have from God? and ye are not your own." "If any man defile the temple of God, him shall God destroy; for the temple of God is holy, which temple ye are." 1 Corinthians 6:19, R.V., margin; 3:17.

Let pupils be impressed with the thought that the body is a temple in which God desires to dwell, that it must be kept pure, the abiding place of high and noble thoughts. As in the study of physiology they see that they are indeed "fearfully and wonderfully made" (Psalm 139:14), they will be inspired with reverence. Instead of marring God's handiwork, they will have an ambition to make all that is possible of themselves, in order to fulfill the Creator's glorious plan. Thus they will come to regard obedience to the laws of health, not as a matter of sacrifice or self-denial, but as it really is, an inestimable privilege and blessing.

22
Temperance and Dietics

"Every man that striveth for the mastery is temperate in all things."

Every student needs to understand the relation between plain living and high thinking. It rests with us individually to decide whether our lives shall be controlled by the mind or by the body. The youth must, each for himself, make the choice that shapes his life; and no pains should be spared that he may understand the forces with which he has to deal, and the influences which mold character and destiny.

Intemperance is a foe against which all need to be guarded. The rapid increase of this terrible evil should arouse every lover of his race to warfare against it. The practice of giving instruction on temperance topics in the schools is a move in the right direction. Instruction in this line should be given in every school and in every home. The youth and children should understand the effect of alcohol, tobacco, and other like poisons in breaking down the body, beclouding the mind, and sensualizing the soul. It should be made plain that no one who uses these things can long possess the full strength of his physical, mental, or moral faculties.

But in order to reach the root of intemperance we must go deeper than the use of alcohol or tobacco. Idleness, lack of aim, or evil associations, may be the predisposing cause. Often it is found at the home table, in families that account themselves strictly temperate. Anything that disorders digestion, that creates undue mental excitement, or in any way enfeebles the system, disturbing the balance of the mental and the physical powers, weakens the control of the mind over the body, and thus tends toward intemperance. The downfall of many a promising youth might be traced to unnatural appetites created by an unwholesome diet.

Tea and coffee, condiments, confectionery, and pastries are all active causes of indigestion. Flesh food also is harmful. Its naturally stimulating effect should be a sufficient argument against its use; and the almost universally diseased condition of animals makes it doubly objectionable. It tends to irritate the nerves and to excite the passions, thus giving the balance of power to the lower propensities.

Those who accustom themselves to a rich, stimulating diet, find after a time that the stomach is not satisfied with simple food. It demands that which is more and more highly seasoned, pungent, and stimulating. As the nerves become disordered and the system weakened, the will seems powerless to resist the unnatural craving. The delicate coating of the stomach becomes irritated and inflamed until the most stimulating food fails of giving relief. A thirst is created that nothing but strong drink will quench.

It is the beginnings of evil that should be guarded against. In the instruction of the youth the effect of apparently small deviations from the right should be made very plain. Let the student be taught the value of a simple, healthful diet in preventing the desire for unnatural stimulants. Let the habit of self-control be early established. Let the youth be impressed with the thought that they are to be masters, and not slaves. Of the kingdom within them God has made them rulers, and they are to exercise their Heaven-appointed kingship. When such instruction is faithfully given, the results will extend far beyond the youth themselves. Influences will reach out that will save thousands of men and women who are on the very brink of ruin.

Diet and Mental Development

The relation of diet to intellectual development should be given far more attention than it has received. Mental confusion and dullness are often the result of errors in diet.

It is frequently urged that, in the selection of food, appetite is a safe guide. If the laws of health had always been obeyed, this would be true. But through wrong habits, continued from generation to generation, appetite has become so perverted that it is constantly craving some hurtful gratification. As a guide it cannot now be trusted.

In the study of hygiene, students should be taught the nutrient value of different foods. The effect of a concentrated and stimulating diet, also of foods deficient in the elements of nutrition, should be made plain. Tea and coffee, fine-flour bread, pickles, coarse vegetables, candies, condiments, and pastries fail of supplying proper nutriment. Many a student has broken down as the result of using such foods. Many a puny child, incapable of vigorous effort of mind or body, is the victim of an impoverished diet. Grains, fruits, nuts, and vegetables, in proper combination, contain all the elements of nutrition; and when properly prepared, they constitute the diet that best promotes both physical and mental strength.

There is need to consider not only the properties of the food but its adaptation to the eater. Often food that can be eaten freely by persons engaged in physical labor must be avoided by those whose work is chiefly mental. Attention should be given also to the proper combination of foods. By brain workers and others of sedentary pursuits, but few kinds should be taken at a meal.

And overeating, even of the most wholesome food, is to be guarded against. Nature can use no more than is required for building up the various organs of the body, and excess clogs the system. Many a student is supposed to have broken down from overstudy, when the real cause was overeating. While proper attention is given to the laws of health, there is little danger from mental taxation; but in many cases of so-called mental failure it is the overcrowding of the stomach that wearies the body and weakens the mind.

In most cases two meals a day are preferable to three. Supper, when taken at an early hour, interferes with the digestion of the previous meal. When taken later, it is not itself digested before bedtime. Thus the stomach fails of securing proper rest. The sleep is disturbed, the brain and nerves are wearied, the appetite for breakfast is impaired, the whole system is unrefreshed and is unready for the day's duties.

The importance of regularity in the time for eating and sleeping should not be overlooked. Since the work of building up the body takes place during the hours of rest, it is essential, especially in youth, that sleep should be regular and abundant.

So far as possible we should avoid hurried eating. The shorter the time for a meal, the less should be eaten. It is better to omit a meal than to eat without proper mastication.

Mealtime should be a season for social intercourse and refreshment. Everything that can burden or irritate should be banished. Let trust and kindliness and gratitude to the Giver of all good be cherished, and the conversation will be cheerful, a pleasant flow of thought that will uplift without wearying.

The observance of temperance and regularity in all things has a wonderful power. It will do more than circumstances or natural endowments in promoting that sweetness and serenity of disposition which count so much in smoothing life's pathway. At the same time the power of self-control thus acquired will be found one of the most valuable of equipments for grappling successfully with the stern duties and realities that await every human being.

Wisdom's "ways are ways of pleasantness, and all her paths are peace." Proverbs 3:17. Let every youth in our land, with the possibilities before him of a destiny higher than that of crowned kings, ponder the lesson conveyed in the words of the wise man, "Blessed art thou, O land, when ... thy princes eat in due season, for strength, and not for drunkenness!" Ecclesiastes 10:17.

23
Recreation

"To everything there is a season."

There is a distinction between recreation and amusement. Recreation, when true to its name, re-creation, tends to strengthen and build up. Calling us aside from our ordinary cares and occupations, it affords refreshment for mind and body, and thus enables us to return with new vigor to the earnest work of life. Amusement, on the other hand, is sought for the sake of pleasure and is often carried to excess; it absorbs the energies that are required for useful work and thus proves a hindrance to life's true success.

The whole body is designed for action; and unless the physical powers are kept in health by active exercise, the mental powers cannot long be used to their highest capacity. The physical inaction which seems almost inevitable in the schoolroom—together with other unhealthful conditions—makes it a trying place for children, especially for those of feeble constitution. Often the ventilation is insufficient. Ill-formed seats encourage unnatural positions, thus cramping the action of the lungs and the heart. Here little children have to spend from three to five hours a day, breathing air that is laden with impurity and perhaps infected with the germs of disease. No wonder that in the schoolroom the foundation of lifelong illness is so often laid. The brain, the most delicate of all the physical organs, and that from which the nervous energy of the whole system is derived, suffers the greatest injury. By being forced into premature or excessive activity, and this under unhealthful conditions, it is enfeebled, and often the evil results are permanent.

Children should not be long confined within doors, nor should they be required to apply themselves closely to study until a good foundation has been laid for physical development. For the first eight or ten years of a child's life the field or garden is the best schoolroom, the mother the best teacher, nature the best lesson book. Even when the child is old enough to attend school, his health should be regarded as of greater importance than a knowledge of books. He should be surrounded with the conditions most favorable to both physical and mental growth.

The child is not alone in the danger from want of air and exercise. In the higher as well as the lower schools these essentials to health are still too often neglected. Many a student sits day after day in a close room bending over his books, his chest so contracted that he cannot take a full, deep breath, his blood moving sluggishly, his feet cold, his head hot. The body not being sufficiently nourished, the muscles are weakened, and the whole system is enervated and diseased. Often such students become lifelong invalids. They might have come from school with increased physical as well as mental strength, had they pursued their studies under proper conditions, with regular exercise in the sunlight and the open air.

The student who with limited time and means is struggling to gain an education should realize that time spent in physical exercise is not lost. He who continually pores over his books will find, after a time, that the mind has lost its freshness. Those who give proper attention to physical development will make greater advancement in literary lines than they would if their entire time were devoted to study.

By pursuing one line of thought exclusively, the mind often becomes unbalanced. But every faculty may be safely exercised if the mental and physical powers are equally taxed and the subjects of thought are varied.

Physical inaction lessens not only mental but moral power. The brain nerves that connect with the whole system are the medium through which heaven communicates with man and affects the inmost life. Whatever hinders the circulation of the electric current in the nervous system, thus weakening the vital powers and lessening mental susceptibility, makes it more difficult to arouse the moral nature.

Again, excessive study, by increasing the flow of blood to the brain, creates morbid excitability that tends to lessen the power of self-control, and too often gives sway to impulse or caprice. Thus the door is opened to impurity. The misuse or nonuse of the physical powers is largely responsible for the tide of corruption that is overspreading the world. "Pride, fullness of bread, and abundance of idleness," are as deadly foes to human progress in this generation as when they led to the destruction of Sodom.

Teachers should understand these things, and should instruct their pupils in these lines. Teach the students that right living depends on right thinking, and that physical activity is essential to purity of thought.

The question of suitable recreation for their pupils is one that teachers often find perplexing. Gymnastic exercises fill a useful place in many schools; but without careful supervision they are often carried to excess. In the gymnasium many youth, by their attempted feats of strength, have done themselves lifelong injury.

Exercise in a gymnasium, however well conducted, cannot supply the place of recreation in the open air, and for this our schools should afford better opportunity. Vigorous exercise the pupils must have. Few evils are more to be dreaded than indolence and aimlessness. Yet the tendency of most athletic sports is a subject of anxious thought to those who have at heart the well-being of the youth. Teachers are troubled as they consider the influence of these sports both on the student's progress in school and on his success in afterlife. The games that occupy so much of his time are diverting the mind from study. They are not helping to prepare the youth for practical, earnest work in life. Their influence does not tend toward refinement, generosity, or real manliness.

Some of the most popular amusements, such as football and boxing, have become schools of brutality. They are developing the same characteristics as did the games of ancient Rome. The love of domination, the pride in mere brute force, the reckless disregard of life, are exerting upon the youth a power to demoralize that is appalling.

Other athletic games, though not so brutalizing, are scarcely less objectionable because of the excess to which they are carried. They stimulate the love of pleasure and excitement, thus fostering a distaste for useful labor, a disposition to shun practical duties and responsibilities. They tend to destroy a relish for life's sober realities and its tranquil enjoyments. Thus the door is opened to dissipation and lawlessness, with their terrible results.

As ordinarily conducted, parties of pleasure also are a hindrance to real growth, either of mind or of character. Frivolous associations, habits of extravagance, of pleasure seeking, and too often of dissipation, are formed, that shape the whole life for evil. In place of such amusements, parents and teachers can do much to supply diversions wholesome and life-giving.

In this, as in all things else that concern our well-being, Inspiration has pointed the way. In early ages, with the people who were under God's direction, life was simple. They lived close to the heart of nature. Their children shared in the labor of the parents and studied the beauties and mysteries of nature's treasure house. And in the quiet of field and wood they pondered those mighty truths handed down as a sacred trust from generation to generation. Such training produced strong men.

In this age, life has become artificial, and men have degenerated. While we may not return fully to the simple habits of those early times, we may learn from them lessons that will make our seasons of recreation what the name implies—seasons of true upbuilding for body and mind and soul.

With the question of recreation the surroundings of the home and the school have much to do. In the choice of a home or the location of a school these things should be considered. Those with whom mental and physical well-being is of greater moment than money or the claims and customs of society, should seek for their children the benefit of nature's teaching, and recreation amidst her surroundings. It would be a great aid in educational work could every school be so situated as to afford the pupils land for cultivation, and access to the fields and woods.

In lines of recreation for the student the best results will be attained through the personal co-operation of the teacher. The true teacher can impart to his pupils few gifts so valuable as the gift of his own companionship. It is true of men and women, and how much more of youth and children, that only as we come in touch through sympathy can we understand them; and we need to understand in order most effectively to benefit. To strengthen the tie of sympathy between teacher and student there are few means that count so much as pleasant association together outside the schoolroom. In some schools the teacher is always with his pupils in their hours or recreation. He unites in their pursuits, accompanies them in their excursions, and seems to make himself one with them. Well would it be for our schools were this practice more generally followed. The sacrifice demanded of the teacher would be great, but he would reap a rich reward.

No recreation helpful only to themselves will prove so great a blessing to the children and youth as that which makes them helpful to others. Naturally enthusiastic and impressible, the young are quick to respond to suggestion. In planning for the culture of plants, let the teacher seek to awaken an interest in beautifying the school grounds and the schoolroom. A double benefit will result. That which the pupils seek to beautify they will be unwilling to have marred or defaced. A refined taste, a love of order, and a habit of caretaking will be encouraged; and the spirit of fellowship and co-operation developed will prove to the pupils a lifelong blessing.

So also a new interest may be given to the work of the garden or the excursion in field or wood, as the pupils are encouraged to remember those shut in from these pleasant places and to share with them the beautiful things of nature.

The watchful teacher will find many opportunities for directing pupils to acts of helpfulness. By little children especially the teacher is regarded with almost unbounded confidence and respect. Whatever he may suggest as to ways of helping in the home, faithfulness in the daily tasks, ministry to the sick or the poor, can hardly fail of bringing forth fruit. And thus again a double gain will be secured. The kindly suggestion will react upon its author. Gratitude and co-operation on the part of the parents will lighten the teacher's burden and brighten his path.

Attention to recreation and physical culture will at times, no doubt, interrupt the regular routine of school-work; but the interruption will prove no real hindrance. In the invigoration of mind and body, the fostering of an unselfish spirit, and the binding together of pupil and teacher by the ties of common interest and friendly association, the expenditure of time and effort will be repaid a hundredfold. A blessed outlet will be afforded for that restless energy which is so often a source of danger to the young. As a safeguard against evil, the preoccupation of the mind with good is worth more than unnumbered barriers of law and discipline.

24
Manual Training

"Study . . . to work with your own hands."

At the creation, labor was appointed as a blessing. It meant development, power, happiness. The changed condition of the earth through the curse of sin has brought a change in the conditions of labor; yet though now attended with anxiety, weariness, and pain, it is still a source of happiness and development. And it is a safeguard against temptation. Its discipline places a check on self-indulgence, and promotes industry, purity, and firmness. Thus it becomes a part of God's great plan for our recovery from the Fall.

The youth should be led to see the true dignity of labor. Show them that God is a constant worker. All things in nature do their allotted work. Action pervades the whole creation, and in order to fulfill our mission we, too, must be active.

In our labor we are to be workers together with God. He gives us the earth and its treasures; but we must adapt them to our use and comfort. He causes the trees to grow; but we prepare the timber and build the house. He has hidden in the earth the gold and silver, the iron and coal; but it is only through toil that we can obtain them.

Show that, while God has created and constantly controls all things, He has endowed us with a power not wholly unlike His. To us has been given a degree of control over the forces of nature. As God called forth the earth in its beauty out of chaos, so we can bring order and beauty out of confusion. And though all things are now marred with evil, yet in our completed work we feel a joy akin to His, when, looking on the fair earth, He pronounced it "very good."

As a rule, the exercise most beneficial to the youth will be found in useful employment. The little child finds both diversion and development in play; and his sports should be such as to promote not only physical, but mental and spiritual growth. As he gains strength and intelligence, the best recreation will be found in some line of effort that is useful. That which trains the hand to helpfulness, and teaches the young to bear their share of life's burdens, is most effective in promoting the growth of mind and character.

The youth need to be taught that life means earnest work, responsibility, care-taking. They need a training that will make them practical—men and women who can cope with emergencies. They should be taught that the discipline of systematic, well-regulated labor is essential, not only as a safeguard against the vicissitudes of life, but as an aid to all-around development.

Notwithstanding all that has been said and written concerning the dignity of labor, the feeling prevails that it is degrading. Young men are anxious to become teachers, clerks, merchants, physicians, lawyers, or to occupy some other position that does not require physical toil. Young women shun housework and seek an education in other lines. These need to learn that no man or woman is degraded by honest toil. That which degrades is idleness and selfish dependence. Idleness fosters self-indulgence, and the result is a life empty and barren—a field inviting the growth of every evil. "The earth which drinketh in the rain that cometh oft upon it, and bringeth forth herbs meet for them by whom it is dressed, receiveth blessing from God: but that which beareth thorns and briers is rejected, and is nigh unto cursing; whose end is to be burned." Hebrews 6:7, 8.

Many of the branches of study that consume the student's time are not essential to usefulness or happiness; but it is essential for every youth to have a thorough acquaintance with everyday duties. If need be, a young woman can dispense with a knowledge of French and algebra, or even of the piano; but it is indispensable that she learn to make good bread, to fashion neatly-fitting garments, and to perform efficiently the many duties that pertain to homemaking.

To the health and happiness of the whole family nothing is more vital than skill and intelligence on the part of the cook. By ill-prepared, unwholesome food she may hinder and even ruin both the adult's usefulness and the child's development. Or by providing food adapted to the needs of the body, and at the same time inviting and palatable, she can accomplish as much in the right as otherwise she accomplishes in the wrong direction. So, in many ways, life's happiness is bound up with faithfulness in common duties.

Since both men and women have a part in home-making, boys as well as girls should gain a knowledge of household duties. To make a bed and put a room in order, to wash dishes, to prepare a meal, to wash and repair his own clothing, is a training that need not make any boy less manly; it will make him happier and more useful. And if girls, in turn, could learn to harness and drive a horse, and to use the saw and the hammer, as well as to rake and the hoe, they would be better fitted to meet the emergencies of life.

Let the children and youth learn from the Bible how God has honored the work of the everyday toiler. Let them read of "the sons of the prophets" (2 Kings 6:1-7), students at school, who were building a house for themselves, and for whom a miracle was wrought to save from loss the ax that was borrowed. Let them read of Jesus the carpenter, and Paul the tentmaker, who with the toil of the craftsman linked the highest ministry, human and divine. Let them read of the lad whose five loaves were used by the Saviour in that wonderful miracle for the feeding of the multitude; of Dorcas the seamstress, called back from death, that she might continue to make garments for the poor; of the wise woman described in the Proverbs, who "seeketh wool and flax, and worketh willingly with her hands;" who "giveth meat to her household, and their task to her maidens;" who "planteth a vineyard," and strengtheneth her arms;" who "stretcheth out her hand to the poor; yea, . . . reacheth forth her hands to the needy;" who "looketh well to the ways of her household, and eateth not the bread of idleness." Proverbs 31:13, 15, R.V.; 31:16, 17, 20, 27.

Of such a one, God says: "She shall be praised. Give her of the fruit of her hands; and let her own works praise her in the gates." Proverbs 31:30, 31.

For every child the first industrial school should be the home. And, so far as possible, facilities for manual training should be connected with every school. To a great degree such training would supply the place of the gymnasium, with the additional benefit of affording valuable discipline.

Manual training is deserving of far more attention than it has received. Schools should be established that, in addition to the highest mental and moral culture, shall provide the best possible facilities for physical development and industrial training. Instruction should be given in agriculture, manufactures—covering as many as possible of the most useful trades—also in household economy, healthful cookery, sewing, hygienic dressmaking, the treatment of the sick, and kindred lines. Gardens, workshops, and treatment rooms should be provided, and the work in every line should be under the direction of skilled instructors.

The work should have a definite aim and should be thorough. While every person needs some knowledge of different handicrafts, it is indispensable that he become proficient in at least one. Every youth, on leaving school, should have acquired a knowledge of some trade or occupation by which, if need be, he may earn a livelihood.

The objection most often urged against industrial training in the schools is the large outlay involved. But the object to be gained is worthy of its cost. No other work committed to us is so important as the training of the youth, and every outlay demanded for its right accomplishment is means well spent.

Even from the viewpoint of financial results, the outlay required for manual training would prove the truest economy. Multitudes of our boys would thus be kept from the street corner and the groggery; the expenditure for gardens, workshops, and baths would be more than met by the saving on hospitals and reformatories. And the youth themselves, trained to habits of industry, and skilled in lines of useful and productive labor—who can estimate their value to society and to the nation?

As a relaxation from study, occupations pursued in the open air, and affording exercise for the whole body, are the most beneficial. No line of manual training is of more value than agriculture. A greater effort should be made to create and to encourage an interest in agricultural pursuits. Let the teacher call attention to what the Bible says about agriculture: that it was God's plan for man to till the earth; that the first man, the ruler of the whole world, was given a garden to cultivate; and that many of the world's greatest men, its real nobility, have been tillers of the soil. Show the opportunities in such a life. The wise man says, "The king himself is served by the field." Ecclesiastes 5:9. Of him who cultivates the soil the Bible declares, "His God doth instruct him to discretion, and doth teach him." Isaiah 28:26. And again, "Whoso keepeth the fig tree shall eat the fruit thereof." Proverbs 27:18. He who earns his livelihood by agriculture escapes many temptations and enjoys unnumbered privileges and blessings denied to those whose work lies in the great cities. And in these days of mammoth trusts and business competition, there are few who enjoy so real an independence and so great certainty of fair return for their labor as does the tiller of the soil.

In the study of agriculture, let pupils be given not only theory, but practice. While they learn what science can teach in regard to the nature and preparation of the soil, the value of different crops, and the best methods of production, let them put their knowledge to use. Let teachers share the work with the students, and show what results can be achieved through skillful, intelligent effort. Thus may be awakened a genuine interest, an ambition to do the work in the best possible manner. Such an ambition, together with the invigorating effect of exercise, sunshine, and pure air, will create a love for agricultural labor that with many youth will determine their choice of an occupation. Thus might be set on foot influences that would go far in turning the tide of migration which now sets so strongly toward the great cities.

Thus, also, our schools could aid effectively in the disposition of the unemployed masses. Thousands of helpless and starving beings, whose numbers are daily swelling the ranks of the criminal classes, might achieve self-support in a happy, healthy, independent life if they could be directed in skillful, diligent labor in the tilling of the soil.

The benefit of manual training is needed also by professional men. A man may have a brilliant mind; he may be quick to catch ideas; his knowledge and skill may secure for him admission to his chosen calling; yet he may still be far from possessing a fitness for its duties. An education derived chiefly from books leads to superficial thinking. Practical work encourages close observation and independent thought. Rightly performed, it tends to develop that practical wisdom which we call common sense. It develops ability to plan and execute, strengthens courage and perseverance, and calls for the exercise of tact and skill.

The physician who has laid a foundation for his professional knowledge by actual service in the sickroom will have a quickness of insight, an all-around knowledge, and an ability in emergencies to render needed service—all essential qualifications, which only a practical training can so fully impart.

The minister, the missionary, the teacher, will find their influence with the people greatly increased when it is manifest that they possess the knowledge and skill required for the practical duties of everyday life. And often the success, perhaps the very life, of the missionary depends on his knowledge of practical things. The ability to prepare food, to deal with accidents and emergencies, to treat disease, to build a house, or a church if need be—often these make all the difference between success and failure in his lifework.

In acquiring an education, many students would gain a most valuable training if they would become self-sustaining. Instead of incurring debts, or depending on the self-denial of their parents, let young men and young women depend on themselves. They will thus learn the value of money, the value of time, strength, and opportunities, and will be under far less temptation to indulge idle and spendthrift habits. The lessons of economy, industry, self-denial, practical business management, and steadfastness of purpose, thus mastered, would prove a most important part of their equipment for the battle of life. And the lesson of self-help learned by the student would go far toward preserving institutions of learning from the burden of debt under which so many schools have struggled, and which has done so much toward crippling their usefulness.

Let the youth be impressed with the thought that education is not to teach them how to escape life's disagreeable tasks and heavy burdens; that its purpose is to lighten the work by teaching better methods and higher aims. Teach them that life's true aim is not to secure the greatest possible gain for themselves, but to honor their Maker in doing their part of the world's work, and lending a helpful hand to those weaker or more ignorant.

One great reason why physical toil is looked down on is the slipshod, unthinking way in which it is so often performed. It is done from necessity, not from choice. The worker puts no heart into it, and he neither preserves self-respect nor wins the respect of others. Manual training should correct this error. It should develop habits of accuracy and thoroughness. Pupils should learn tact and system; they should learn to economize time and to make every move count. They should not only be taught the best methods, but be inspired with ambition constantly to improve. Let it be their aim to make their work as nearly perfect as human brains and hands can make it.

Such training will make the youth masters and not slaves of labor. It will lighten the lot of the hard toiler, and will ennoble even the humblest occupation. He who regards work as mere drudgery, and settles down to it with self-complacent ignorance, making no effort to improve, will find it indeed a burden. But those who recognize science in the humblest work will see in it nobility and beauty, and will take pleasure in performing it with faithfulness and efficiency.

A youth so trained, whatever his calling in life, so long as it is honest, will make his position one of usefulness and honor.

Character Building

"See . . . that thou make all things according to the pattern showed to thee in the mount."

25
Education and Character

"The stability of thy times . . . shall be wisdom and knowledge."

True education does not ignore the value of scientific knowledge or literary acquirements; but above information it values power; above power, goodness; above intellectual acquirements, character. The world does not so much need men of great intellect as of noble character. It needs men in whom ability is controlled by steadfast principle.

"Wisdom is the principal thing; therefore get wisdom." "The tongue of the wise useth knowledge aright." Proverbs 4:7; 15:2. True education imparts this wisdom. It teaches the best use not only of one but of all our powers and acquirements. Thus it covers the whole circle of obligation—to ourselves, to the world, and to God.

Character building is the most important work ever entrusted to human beings; and never before was its diligent study so important as now. Never was any previous generation called to meet issues so momentous; never before were young men and young women confronted by perils so great as confront them today.

At such a time as this, what is the trend of the education given? To what motive is appeal most often made? To self-seeking. Much of the education given is a perversion of the name. In true education the selfish ambition, the greed for power, the disregard for the rights and needs of humanity, that are the curse of our world, find a counterinfluence. God's plan of life has a place for every human being. Each is to improve his talents to the utmost; and faithfulness in doing this, be the gifts few or many, entitles one to honor. In God's plan there is no place for selfish rivalry. Those who measure themselves by themselves, and compare themselves among themselves, are not wise. 2 Corinthians 10:12. Whatever we do is to be done "as of the ability which God giveth." 1 Peter 4:11. It is to be done "heartily, as to the Lord, and not unto men; knowing that of the Lord ye shall receive the reward of the inheritance: for ye serve the Lord Christ." Colossians 3:23, 24. Precious the service done and the education gained in carrying out these principles. But how widely different is much of the education now given! From the child's earliest years it is an appeal to emulation and rivalry; it fosters selfishness, the root of all evil.

Thus is created strife for supremacy; and there is encouraged the system of "cramming," which in so many cases destroys health and unfits for usefulness. In many others, emulation leads to dishonesty; and by fostering ambition and discontent, it embitters the life and helps to fill the world with those restless, turbulent spirits that are a continual menace to society.

Nor does danger pertain to methods only. It is found also in the subject matter of the studies.

What are the works on which, throughout the most susceptible years of life, the minds of the youth are led to dwell? In the study of language and literature, from what fountains are the youth taught to drink?—From the wells of paganism; from springs fed by the corruptions of ancient heathendom. They are bidden to study authors, of whom, without dispute, it is declared that they have no regard for the principles of morality.

And of how many modern authors also might the same be said! With how many are grace and beauty of language but a disguise for principles that in their real deformity would repel the reader!

Besides these there is a multitude of fiction writers, luring to pleasant dreams in palaces of ease. These writers may not be open to the charge of immorality, yet their work is no less really fraught with evil. It is robbing thousands upon thousands of the time and energy and self-discipline demanded by the stern problems of life.

In the study of science, as generally pursued, there are dangers equally great. Evolution and its kindred errors are taught in schools of every grade, from the kindergarten to the college. Thus the study of science, which should impart a knowledge of God, is so mingled with the speculations and theories of men that it tends to infidelity.

Even Bible study, as too often conducted in the schools, is robbing the world of the priceless treasure of the word of God. The work of "higher criticism," in dissecting, conjecturing, reconstructing, is destroying faith in the Bible as a divine revelation; it is robbing God's word of power to control, uplift, and inspire human lives.

As the youth go out into the world to encounter its allurements to sin—the passion for money getting, for amusement and indulgence, for display, luxury, and extravagance, the overreaching, fraud, robbery, and ruin—what are the teachings there to be met?

Spiritualism asserts that men are unfallen demigods; that "each mind will judge itself;" that "true knowledge places men above all law;" that "all sins committed are innocent;" for "whatever is, is right," and "God doth not condemn." The basest of human beings it represents as in heaven, and highly exalted there. Thus it declares to all men, "It matters not what you do; live as you please, heaven is your home." Multitudes are thus led to believe that desire is the highest law, that license is liberty, and that man is accountable only to himself.

With such teaching given at the very outset of life, when impulse is strongest, and the demand for self-restraint and purity is most urgent, where are the safeguards of virtue? what is to prevent the world from becoming a second Sodom?

At the same time anarchy is seeking to sweep away all law, not only divine, but human. The centralizing of wealth and power; the vast combinations for the enriching of the few at the expense of the many; the combinations of the poorer classes for the defense of their interests and claims; the spirit of unrest, of riot and bloodshed; the world-wide dissemination of the same teachings that led to the French Revolution—all are tending to involve the whole world in a struggle similar to that which convulsed France.

Such are the influences to be met by the youth of today. To stand amidst such upheavals they are now to lay the foundations of character.

In every generation and in every land the true foundation and pattern for character building have been the same. The divine law, "Thou shalt love the Lord thy God with all thy heart; . . . and thy neighbor as thyself" (Luke 10:27), the great principle made manifest in the character and life of our Saviour, is the only secure foundation and the only sure guide.

"The stability of thy times and the strength of thy happiness shall be wisdom and knowledge" (Isaiah 33:6, Leeser's translation)—that wisdom and knowledge which God's word alone can impart.

It is as true now as when the words were spoken to Israel of obedience to His commandments: "This is your wisdom and your understanding in the sight of the nations." Deuteronomy 4:6.

Here is the only safeguard for individual integrity, for the purity of the home, the well-being of society, or the stability of the nation. Amidst all life's perplexities and dangers and conflicting claims the one safe and sure rule is to do what God says. "The statutes of the Lord are right," and "he that doeth these things shall never be moved." Psalms 19:8; 15:5.

26
Methods of Teaching

"To give prudence to the simple, to the young man knowledge and discretion."

For ages education has had to do chiefly with the memory. This faculty has been taxed to the utmost, while the other mental powers have not been correspondingly developed. Students have spent their time in laboriously crowding the mind with knowledge, very little of which could be utilized. The mind thus burdened with that which it cannot digest and assimilate is weakened; it becomes incapable of vigorous, self-reliant effort, and is content to depend on the judgment and perception of others.

Seeing the evils of this method, some have gone to another extreme. In their view, man needs only to develop that which is within him. Such education leads the student to self-sufficiency, thus cutting him off from the source of true knowledge and power.

The education that consists in the training of the memory, tending to discourage independent thought, has a moral bearing which is too little appreciated. As the student sacrifices the power to reason and judge for himself, he becomes incapable of discriminating between truth and error, and falls an easy prey to deception. He is easily led to follow tradition and custom.

It is a fact widely ignored, though never without danger, that error rarely appears for what it really is. It is by mingling with or attaching itself to truth that it gains acceptance. The eating of the tree of knowledge of good and evil caused the ruin of our first parents, and the acceptance of a mingling of good and evil is the ruin of men and women today. The mind that depends upon the judgment of others is certain, sooner or later, to be misled.

The power to discriminate between right and wrong we can possess only through individual dependence upon God. Each for himself is to learn from Him through His word. Our reasoning powers were given us for use, and God desires them to be exercised. "Come now, and let us reason together" (Isaiah 1:18), He invites us. In reliance upon Him we may have wisdom to "refuse the evil, and choose the good." Isaiah 7:15; James 1:5.

In all true teaching the personal element is essential. Christ in His teaching dealt with men individually. It was by personal contact and association that He trained the Twelve. It was in private, often to but one listener, that He gave His most precious instruction. To the honored rabbi at the night conference on the Mount of Olives, to the despised woman at the well of Sychar, He opened His richest treasures; for in these hearers He discerned the impressible heart, the open mind, the receptive spirit. Even the crowd that so often thronged His steps was not to Christ an indiscriminate mass of human beings. He spoke directly to every mind and appealed to every heart. He watched the faces of His hearers, marked the lighting up of the countenance, the quick, responsive glance, which told that truth had reached the soul; and there vibrated in His heart the answering chord of sympathetic joy.

Christ discerned the possibilities in every human being. He was not turned aside by an unpromising exterior or by unfavorable surroundings. He called Matthew from the tollbooth, and Peter and his brethren from the fishing boat, to learn of Him.

The same personal interest, the same attention to individual development, are needed in educational work today. Many apparently unpromising youth are richly endowed with talents that are put to no use. Their faculties lie hidden because of a lack of discernment on the part of their educators. In many a boy or girl outwardly as unattractive as a rough-hewn stone, may be found precious material that will stand the test of heat and storm and pressure. The true educator, keeping in view what his pupils may become, will recognize the value of the material upon which he is working. He will take a personal interest in each pupil and will seek to develop all his powers. However imperfect, every effort to conform to right principles will be encouraged.

Every youth should be taught the necessity and the power of application. Upon this, far more than upon genius or talent, does success depend. Without application the most brilliant talents avail little, while with rightly directed effort persons of very ordinary natural abilities have accomplished wonders. And genius, at whose achievements we marvel, is almost invariably united with untiring, concentrated effort.

The youth should be taught to aim at the development of all their faculties, the weaker as well as the stronger. With many there is a disposition to restrict their study to certain lines, for which they have a natural liking. This error should be guarded against. The natural aptitudes indicate the direction of the lifework, and, when legitimate, should be carefully cultivated. At the same time it must be kept in mind that a well-balanced character and efficient work in any line depend, to a great degree, on that symmetrical development which is the result of thorough, all-round training.

The teacher should constantly aim at simplicity and effectiveness. He should teach largely by illustration, and even in dealing with older pupils should be careful to make every explanation plain and clear. Many pupils well advanced in years are but children in understanding.

An important element in educational work is enthusiasm. On this point there is a useful suggestion in a remark once made by a celebrated actor. The archbishop of Canterbury had put to him the question why actors in a play affect their audiences so powerfully by speaking of things imaginary, while ministers of the gospel often affect theirs so little by speaking of things real. "With due submission to your grace," replied the actor, "permit me to say that the reason is plain: It lies in the power of enthusiasm. We on the stage speak of things imaginary as if they were real, and you in the pulpit speak of things real as if they were imaginary."

The teacher in his work is dealing with things real, and he should speak of them with all the force and enthusiasm which a knowledge of their reality and importance can inspire.

Every teacher should see to it that his work tends to definite results. Before attempting to teach a subject, he should have a distinct plan in mind, and should know just what he desires to accomplish. He should not rest satisfied with the presentation of any subject until the student understands the principle involved, perceives its truth, and is able to state clearly what he has learned.

So long as the great purpose of education is kept in view, the youth should be encouraged to advance just as far as their capabilities will permit. But before taking up the higher branches of study, let them master the lower. This is too often neglected. Even among students in the higher schools and the colleges there is great deficiency in knowledge of the common branches of education. Many students devote their time to higher mathematics when they are incapable of keeping simple accounts. Many study elocution with a view to acquiring the graces of oratory when they are unable to read in an intelligible and impressive manner. Many who have finished the study of rhetoric fail in the composition and spelling of an ordinary letter.

A thorough knowledge of the essentials of education should be not only the condition of admission to a higher course, but the constant test for continuance and advancement.

And in every branch of education there are objects to be gained more important than those secured by mere technical knowledge. Take language, for example. More important than the acquirement of foreign languages, living or dead, is the ability to write and speak one's mother tongue with ease and accuracy; but no training gained through a knowledge of grammatical rules can compare in importance with the study of language from a higher point of view. With this study, to a great degree, is bound up life's weal or woe.

The chief requisite of language is that it be pure and kind and true—"the outward expression of an inward grace." God says: "Whatsoever things are true, whatsoever things are honest, whatsoever things are just, whatsoever things are pure, whatsoever things are lovely, whatsoever things are of good report; if there be any virtue, and if there be any praise, think on these things." Philippians 4:8. And if such are the thoughts, such will be the expression.

The best school for this language study is the home; but since the work of the home is so often neglected, it devolves on the teacher to aid his pupils in forming right habits of speech.

The teacher can do much to discourage that evil habit, the curse of the community, the neighborhood, and the home—the habit of backbiting, gossip, ungenerous criticism. In this no pains should be spared. Impress upon the students the fact that this habit reveals a lack of culture and refinement and of true goodness of heart; it unfits one both for the society of the truly cultured and refined in this world and for association with the holy ones of heaven.

We think with horror of the cannibal who feasts on the still warm and trembling flesh of his victim; but are the results of even this practice more terrible than are the agony and ruin caused by misrepresenting motive, blackening reputation, dissecting character? Let the children, and the youth as well, learn what God says about these things:

"Death and life are in the power of the tongue." Proverbs 18:21.

In Scripture, backbiters are classed with "haters of God," with "inventors of evil things," with those who are "without natural affection, implacable, unmerciful," "full of envy, murder, debate, deceit, malignity." It is "the judgment of God, that they which commit such things are worthy of death." Romans 1:30, 31, 29, 32. He whom God accounts a citizen of Zion is he that "speaketh the truth in his heart;" "that backbiteth not with his tongue," "nor taketh up a reproach against his neighbor." Psalm 15:2, 3.

God's word condemns also the use of those meaningless phrases and expletives that border on profanity. It condemns the deceptive compliments, the evasions of truth, the exaggerations, the misrepresentations in trade, that are current in society and in the business world. "Let your speech be, Yea, yea; Nay, nay: and whatsoever is more than these is of the evil one." Matthew 5:37, R.V.

"As a madman who casteth firebrands, arrows, and death, so is the man that deceiveth his neighbor, and saith, Am not I in sport?" Proverbs 26:18, 19.

Closely allied to gossip is the covert insinuation, the sly innuendo, by which the unclean in heart seek to insinuate the evil they dare not openly express. Every approach to these practices the youth should be taught to shun as they would shun the leprosy.

In the use of language there is perhaps no error that old and young are more ready to pass over lightly in themselves than hasty, impatient speech. They think it a sufficient excuse to plead, "I was off my guard, and did not really mean what I said." But God's word does not treat it lightly. The Scripture says:

"Seest thou a man that is hasty in his words? there is more hope of a fool than of him." Proverbs 29:20.

"He that hath no rule over his own spirit is like a city that is broken down, and without walls." Proverbs 25:28.

In one moment, by the hasty, passionate, careless tongue, may be wrought evil that a whole lifetime's repentance cannot undo. Oh, the hearts that are broken, the friends estranged, the lives wrecked, by the harsh, hasty words of those who might have brought help and healing!

"There is that speaketh like the piercings of a sword: but the tongue of the wise is health." Proverbs 12:18.

One of the characteristics that should be especially cherished and cultivated in every child is that self-forgetfulness which imparts to the life such an unconscious grace. Of all excellences of character this is one of the most beautiful, and for every true lifework it is one of the qualifications most essential.

Children need appreciation, sympathy, and encouragement, but care should be taken not to foster in them a love of praise. It is not wise to give them special notice, or to repeat before them their clever sayings. The parent or teacher who keeps in view the true ideal of character and the possibilities of achievement, cannot cherish or encourage self-sufficiency. He will not encourage in the youth the desire or effort to display their ability or proficiency. He who looks higher than himself will be humble; yet he will possess a dignity that is not abashed or disconcerted by outward display or human greatness.

It is not by arbitrary law or rule that the graces of character are developed. It is by dwelling in the atmosphere of the pure, the noble, the true. And wherever there is purity of heart and nobleness of character, it will be revealed in purity and nobleness of action and of speech.

"He that loveth pureness of heart, for the grace of his lips the King shall be his friend." Proverbs 22:11.

As with language, so with every other study; it may be so conducted that it will tend to the strengthening and upbuilding of character.

Of no study is this true to a greater degree than of history. Let it be considered from the divine point of view.

As too often taught, history is little more than a record of the rise and fall of kings, the intrigues of courts, the victories and defeats of armies—a story of ambition and greed, of deception, cruelty, and bloodshed. Thus taught, its results cannot but be detrimental. The heart-sickening reiteration of crimes and atrocities, the enormities, the cruelties portrayed, plant seeds that in many live bring forth fruit in a harvest of evil.

Far better is it to learn, in the light of God's word, the causes that govern the rise and fall of kingdoms. Let the youth study these records, and see how the true prosperity of nations has been bound up with an acceptance of the divine principles. Let him study the history of the great reformatory movements, and see how often these principles, though despised and hated, their advocates brought to the dungeon and the scaffold, have through these very sacrifices triumphed.

Such study will give broad, comprehensive views of life. It will help the youth to understand something of its relations and dependencies, how wonderfully we are bound together in the great brotherhood of society and nations, and to how great an extent the oppression or degradation of one member means loss to all.

In the study of figures the work should be made practical. Let every youth and every child be taught, not merely to solve imaginary problems, but to keep an accurate account of his own income and outgoes. Let him learn the right use of money by using it. Whether supplied by their parents or by their own earnings, let boys and girls learn to select and purchase their own clothing, their books, and other necessities; and by keeping an account of their expenses they will learn, as they could learn in no other way, the value and the use of money. This training will help them to distinguish true economy from niggardliness on the one hand and prodigality on the other. Rightly directed it will encourage habits of benevolence. It will aid the youth in learning to give, not from the mere impulse of the moment, as their feelings are stirred, but regularly and systematically.

In this way every study may become an aid in the solution of that greatest of all problems, the training of men and women for the best discharge of life's responsibilities.

27
Deportment

"Love . . . doth not behave itself unseemly."

The value of courtesy is too little appreciated. Many who are kind at heart lack kindliness of manner. Many who command respect by their sincerity and uprightness are sadly deficient in geniality. This lack mars their own happiness and detracts from their service to others. Many of life's sweetest and most helpful experiences are, often for mere want of thought, sacrificed by the uncourteous.

Cheerfulness and courtesy should especially be cultivated by parents and teachers. All may possess a cheerful countenance, a gentle voice, a courteous manner, and these are elements of power. Children are attracted by a cheerful, sunny demeanor. Show them kindness and courtesy, and they will manifest the same spirit toward you and toward one another.

True courtesy is not learned by the mere practice of rules of etiquette. Propriety of deportment is at all times to be observed; wherever principle is not compromised, consideration of others will lead to compliance with accepted customs; but true courtesy requires no sacrifice of principle to conventionality. It ignores caste. It teaches self-respect, respect for the dignity of man as man, a regard for every member of the great human brotherhood.

There is danger of placing too high a value upon mere manner and form, and devoting too much time to education in these lines. The life is strenuous effort demanded of every youth, the hard, often uncongenial work required even for life's ordinary duties, and much more for lightening the world's heavy burden of ignorance and wretchedness—these give little place for conventionalities.

Many who lay great stress upon etiquette show little respect for anything, however excellent, that fails of meeting their artificial standard. This is false education. It fosters critical pride and narrow exclusiveness.

The essence of true politeness is consideration for others. The essential, enduring education is that which broadens the sympathies and encourages universal kindliness. That so-called culture which does not make a youth deferential toward his parents, appreciative of their excellences, forbearing toward their defects, and helpful to their necessities; which does not make him considerate and tender, generous and helpful toward the young, the old, and the unfortunate, and courteous toward all, is a failure.

Real refinement of thought and manner is better learned in the school of the divine Teacher than by any observance of set rules. His love pervading the heart gives to the character those refining touches that fashion it in the semblance of His own. This education imparts a heaven-born dignity and sense of propriety. It gives a sweetness of disposition and a gentleness of manner that can never be equaled by the superficial polish of fashionable society.

The Bible enjoins courtesy, and it presents many illustrations of the unselfish spirit, the gentle grace, the winsome temper, that characterize true politeness. These are but reflections of the character of Christ. All the real tenderness and courtesy in the world, even among those who do not acknowledge His name, is from Him. And He desires these characteristics to be perfectly reflected in His children. It is His purpose that in us men shall behold His beauty.

The most valuable treatise on etiquette ever penned is the precious instruction given by the Saviour, with the utterance of the Holy Spirit through the apostle Paul—words that should be ineffaceably written in the memory of every human being, young or old:

"As I have loved you, that ye also love one another."
John 13:34.

"Love suffereth long, and is kind;
Love envieth not;
Love vaunteth not itself,
Is not puffed up,
Doth not behave itself unseemly,
Seeketh not its own,
Is not provoked,
Taketh not account of evil;
Rejoiceth not in unrighteousness,
But rejoiceth with the truth;
Beareth all things,
Believeth all things,
Hopeth all things,
Endureth all things.
Love never faileth."

1 Corinthians 13:4-8, R.V.

Another precious grace that should be carefully cherished is reverence. True reverence for God is inspired by a sense of His infinite greatness and a realization of His presence. With this sense of the Unseen the heart of every child should be deeply impressed. The hour and place of prayer and the services of public worship the child should be taught to regard as sacred because God is there. And as reverence is manifested in attitude and demeanor, the feeling that inspires it will be deepened.

Well would it be for young and old to study and ponder and often repeat those words of Holy Writ that show how the place marked by God's special presence should be regarded.

"Put off thy shoes from off thy feet," He commanded Moses at the burning bush; "for the place whereon thou standest is holy ground." Exodus 3:5.

Jacob, after beholding the vision of the angels, exclaimed, "The Lord is in this place; and I knew it not. . . . This is none other but the house of God, and this is the gate of heaven." Genesis 28:16,17.

"The Lord is in His holy temple: let all the earth keep silence before Him." Habakkuk 2:20.

"The Lord is a great God,
And a great King above all gods. . . .
O come, let us worship and bow down:
Let us kneel before the Lord our Maker."
"It is He that hath made us, and not we ourselves;
We are His people, and the sheep of His pasture.
Enter into His gates with thanksgiving,
And into His courts with praise:
Be thankful unto Him, and bless His name."
Psalms 95:3-6; 100:3, 4.

Reverence should be shown also for the name of God. Never should that name be spoken lightly or thoughtlessly. Even in prayer its frequent or needless repetition should be avoided. "Holy and reverend is His name." Psalm 111:9. Angels, as they speak it, veil their faces. With what reverence should we, who are fallen and sinful, take it upon your lips!

We should reverence God's word. For the printed volume we should show respect, never putting it to common uses, or handling it carelessly. And never should Scripture be quoted in a jest, or paraphrased to point a witty saying. "Every word of God is pure;" "as silver tried in a furnace of earth, purified seven times." Proverbs 30:5; Psalm 12:6.

Above all, let children be taught that true reverence is shown by obedience. God has commanded nothing that is unessential, and there is no other way of manifesting reverence so pleasing to Him as obedience to that which He has spoken.

Reverence should be shown for God's representatives—for ministers, teachers, and parents who are called to speak and act in His stead. In the respect shown to them He is honored.

And God has especially enjoined tender respect toward the aged. He says, "The hoary head is a crown of glory, if it be found in the way of righteousness." Proverbs 16:31. It tells of battles fought, and victories gained; of burdens borne, and temptations resisted. It tells of weary feet nearing their rest, of places soon to be vacant. Help the children to think of this, and they will smooth the path of the aged by their courtesy and respect, and will bring grace and beauty into their young lives as they heed the command to "rise up before the hoary head, and honor the face of the old man." Leviticus 19:32.

Fathers and mothers and teachers need to appreciate more fully the responsibility and honor that God has place upon them, in making them, to the child, the representatives of Himself. The character revealed in the contact of daily life will interpret to the child, for good or evil, those words of God:

"Like as a father pitieth his children, so the Lord pitieth them that fear Him." Psalm 103:13. "As one whom his mother comforteth, so will I comfort you." Isaiah 66:13.

Happy the child in whom such words as these awaken love and gratitude and trust; the child to whom the tenderness and justice and long-suffering of father and mother and teacher interpret the love and justice and long-suffering of God; the child who by trust and submission and reverence toward his earthly protectors learns to trust and obey and reverence his God. He who imparts to child or pupil such a gift has endowed him with a treasure more precious than the wealth of all the ages—a treasure as enduring as eternity.

28
Relation of Dress to Education

"In modest apparel." "The king's daughter is all glorious within."

No education can be complete that does not teach right principles in regard to dress. Without such teaching, the work of education is too often retarded and perverted. Love of dress, and devotion to fashion, are among the teacher's most formidable rivals and most effective hindrances.

Fashion is a mistress that rules with an iron hand. In very many homes the strength and time and attention of parents and children are absorbed in meeting her demands. The rich are ambitious to outdo one another in conforming to her ever-varying styles; the middle and poorer classes strive to approach the standard set by those supposed to be above them. Where means or strength is limited, and the ambition for gentility is great, the burden becomes almost insupportable.

With many it matters not how becoming, or even beautiful, a garment may be, let the fashion change, and it must be remade or cast aside. The members of the household are doomed to ceaseless toil. There is no time for training the children, no time for prayer or Bible study, no time for helping the little ones to become acquainted with God through His works.

There is no time and no money for charity. And often the home table is stinted. The food is ill selected and hastily prepared, and the demands of nature are but partially supplied. The result is wrong habits of diet, which create disease or lead to intemperance.

The love of display produces extravagance, and in many young people kills the aspiration for a nobler life. Instead of seeking an education, they early engage in some occupation to earn money for indulging the passion for dress. And through this passion many a young girl is beguiled to ruin.

In many a home the family resources are overtaxed. The father, unable to supply the demands of the mother and the children, is tempted to dishonesty, and again dishonor and ruin are the result.

Even the day and the services of worship are not exempt from fashion's domination. Rather they afford opportunity for the greater display of her power. The church is made a parade ground, and the fashions are studied more than the sermon. The poor, unable to meet the demands of custom, stay away from church altogether. The day of rest is spent in idleness, and by the youth often in associations that are demoralizing.

At school, the girls are by unsuitable and uncomfortable clothing unfitted either for study or for recreation. Their minds are preoccupied, and the teacher has a difficult task to awaken their interest.

For breaking the spell of fashion, the teacher can often find no means more effective than contact with nature. Let pupils taste the delights to be found by river or lake or sea; let them climb the hills, gaze on the sunset glory, explore the treasures of wood and field; let them learn the pleasure of cultivating plants and flowers; and the importance of an additional ribbon or ruffle will sink into insignificance.

Lead the youth to see that in dress, as in diet, plain living is indispensable to high thinking. Lead them to see how much there is to learn and to do; how precious are the days of youth as a preparation for the lifework. Help them to see what treasures there are in the word of God, in the book of nature, and in the records of noble lives.

Let their minds be directed to the suffering which they might relieve. Help them to see that by every dollar squandered in display, the spender is deprived of means for feeding the hungry, clothing the naked, and comforting the sorrowful.

They cannot afford to miss life's glorious opportunities, to dwarf their minds, to ruin their health, and to wreck their happiness, for the sake of obedience to mandates that have no foundation in reason, in comfort, or in comeliness.

At the same time the young should be taught to recognize the lesson of nature, "He hath made everything beautiful in its time." Ecclesiastes 3:11, R.V. In dress, as in all things else, it is our privilege to honor our Creator. He desires our clothing to be not only neat and healthful, but appropriate and becoming.

A person's character is judged by his style of dress. A refined taste, a cultivated mind, will be revealed in the choice of simple and appropriate attire. Chaste simplicity in dress, when united with modesty of demeanor, will go far toward surrounding a young woman with that atmosphere of sacred reserve which will be to her a shield from a thousand perils.

Let girls be taught that the art of dressing well includes the ability to make their own clothing. This is an ambition that every girl should cherish. It will be a means of usefulness and independence that she cannot afford to miss.

It is right to love beauty and to desire it; but God desires us to love and to seek first the highest beauty—that which is imperishable. The choicest productions of human skill possess no beauty that can bear comparison with that beauty of character which in His sight is of "great price."

Let the youth and the little children be taught to choose for themselves that royal robe woven in heaven's loom—the "fine linen, clean and white" (Revelation 19:8), which all the holy ones of earth will wear. This robe, Christ's own spotless character, is freely offered to every human being. But all who receive it will receive and wear it here.

Let the children be taught that as they open their minds to pure, loving thoughts and do loving and helpful deeds, they are clothing themselves with His beautiful garment of character. This apparel will make them beautiful and beloved here, and will hereafter be their title of admission to the palace of the King. His promise is:

"They shall walk with Me in white: for they are worthy." Revelation 3:4.

29
The Sabbath

"It is a sign between me and you; . . . that ye may know that I am the Lord."

The value of the Sabbath as a means of education is beyond estimate. Whatever of ours God claims from us, He returns again, enriched, transfigured, with His own glory. The tithe that He claimed from Israel was devoted to preserving among men, in its glorious beauty, the pattern of His temple in the heavens, the token of His presence on the earth. So the portion of our time which He claims is given again to us, bearing His name and seal. "It is a sign," He says, "between Me and you; . . . that ye may know that I am the Lord;" because "in six days the Lord made heaven and earth, the sea, and all that in them is, and rested the seventh day: wherefore the Lord blessed the Sabbath day, and hallowed it." Exodus 31:13; 20:11. The Sabbath is a sign of creative and redeeming power; it points to God as the source of life and knowledge; it recalls man's primeval glory, and thus witnesses to God's purpose to re-create us in His own image.

The Sabbath and the family were alike instituted in Eden, and in God's purpose they are indissolubly linked together. On this day more than on any other, it is possible for us to live the life of Eden. It was God's plan for the members of the family to be associated in work and study, in worship and recreation, the father as priest of his household, and both father and mother as teachers and companions of their children. But the results of sin, having changed the conditions of life, to a great degree prevent this association. Often the father hardly sees the faces of his children throughout the week. He is almost wholly deprived of opportunity for companionship or instruction. But God's love has set a limit to the demands of toil. Over the Sabbath He places His merciful hand. In His own day He preserves for the family opportunity for communion with Him, with nature, and with one another.

Since the Sabbath is the memorial of creative power, it is the day above all others when we should acquaint ourselves with God through His works. In the minds of the children the very thought of the Sabbath should be bound up with the beauty of natural things. Happy is the family who can go to the place of worship on the Sabbath as Jesus and His disciples went to the synagogue—across the fields, along the shores of the lake, or through the groves. Happy the father and mother who can teach their children God's written word with illustrations from the open pages of the book of nature; who can gather under the green trees, in the fresh, pure air, to study the word and to sing the praise of the Father above.

By such associations parents may bind their children to their hearts, and thus to God, by ties that can never be broken.

As a means of intellectual training, the opportunities of the Sabbath are invaluable. Let the Sabbath-school lesson be learned, not by a hasty glance at the lesson scripture on Sabbath morning, but by careful study for the next week on Sabbath afternoon, with daily review or illustration during the week. Thus the lesson will become fixed in the memory, a treasure never to be wholly lost.

In listening to the sermon, let parents and children note the text and the scriptures quoted, and as much as possible of the line of thought, to repeat to one another at home. This will go far toward relieving the weariness with which children so often listen to a sermon, and it will cultivate in all a habit of attention and of connected thought.

Meditation on the themes thus suggested will open to the student treasures of which he has never dreamed. He will prove in his own life the reality of the experience described in the scripture:

"Thy words were found, and I did eat them; and Thy word was unto me the joy and rejoicing of mine heart." Jeremiah 15:16.

"I will meditate in Thy statutes." "More to be desired are they than gold, yea, than much fine gold. . . . Moreover by them is Thy servant warned: and in keeping of them there is great reward." Psalms 119:48; 19:10, 11.

30
Faith and Prayer

"Faith is the assurance of things hoped for."
"Believe that ye receive, . . . and ye shall have."

Faith is trusting God—believing that He loves us and knows best what is for our good. Thus, instead of our own, it leads us to choose His way. In place of our ignorance, it accepts His wisdom; in place of our weakness, His strength; in place of our sinfulness, His righteousness. Our lives, ourselves, are already His; faith acknowledges His ownership and accepts its blessing. Truth, uprightness, purity, have been pointed out as secrets of life's success. It is faith that puts us in possession of these principles.

Every good impulse or aspiration is the gift of God; faith receives from God the life that alone can produce true growth and efficiency.

How to exercise faith should be made very plain. To every promise of God there are conditions. If we are willing to do His will, all His strength is ours. Whatever gift He promises, is in the promise itself. "The seed is the word of God." Luke 8:11. As surely as the oak is in the acorn, so surely is the gift of God in His promise. If we receive the promise, we have the gift.

Faith that enables us to receive God's gifts is itself a gift, of which some measure is imparted to every human being. It grows as exercised in appropriating the word of God. In order to strengthen faith, we must often bring it in contact with the word.

In the study of the Bible the student should be led to see the power of God's word. In the creation, "He spake, and it was done; He commanded, and it stood fast." He "calleth those things which be not as though they were" (Psalm 33:9; Romans 4:17); for when He calls them, they are.

How often those who trusted the word of God, though in themselves utterly helpless, have withstood the power of the whole world—Enoch, pure in heart, holy in life, holding fast his faith in the triumph of righteousness against a corrupt and scoffing generation; Noah and his household against the men of his time, men of the greatest physical and mental strength and the most debased in morals; the children of Israel at the Red Sea, a helpless, terrified multitude of slaves, against the mightiest army of the mightiest nation on the globe; David, a shepherd lad, having God's promise of the throne, against Saul, the established monarch, bent on holding fast his power; Shadrach and his companions in the fire, and Nebuchadnezzar on the throne; Daniel among the lions, his enemies in the high places of the kingdom; Jesus on the cross, and the Jewish priests and rulers forcing even the Roman governor to work their will; Paul in chains led to a criminal's death, Nero the despot of a world empire.

Such examples are not found in the Bible only. They abound in every record of human progress. The Vaudois and the Huguenots, Wycliffe and Huss, Jerome and Luther, Tyndale and Knox, Zinzendorf and Wesley, with multitudes of others, have witnessed to the power of God's word against human power and policy in support of evil. These are the world's true nobility. This is its royal line. In this line the youth of today are called to take their places.

Faith is needed in the smaller no less than in the greater affairs of life. In all our daily interests and occupations the sustaining strength of God becomes real to us through an abiding trust.

Viewed from its human side, life is to all an untried path. It is a path in which, as regards our deeper experiences, we each walk alone. Into our inner life no other human being can fully enter. As the little child sets forth on that journey in which, sooner or later, he must choose his own course, himself deciding life's issues for eternity, how earnest should be the effort to direct his trust to the sure Guide and Helper!

As a shield from temptation and an inspiration to purity and truth, no other influence can equal the sense of God's presence. "All things are naked and opened unto the eyes of Him with whom we have to do." He is "of purer eyes than to behold evil, and canst not look on iniquity." Hebrews 4:13; Habakkuk 1:13. This thought was Joseph's shield amidst the corruptions of Egypt. To the allurements of temptation his answer was steadfast: "How . . . can I do this great wickedness, and sin against God?" Genesis 39:9. Such a shield, faith, if cherished, will bring to every soul.

Only the sense of God's presence can banish the fear that, for the timid child, would make life a burden. Let him fix in his memory the promise, "The angel of the Lord encampeth round about them that fear Him, and delivereth them." Psalm 34:7. Let him read that wonderful story of Elisha in the mountain city, and, between him and the hosts of armed foemen, a mighty encircling band of heavenly angels. Let him read how to Peter, in prison and condemned to death, God's angel appeared; how, past the armed guards, the massive doors and great iron gateway with their bolts and bars, the angel led God's servant forth in safety. Let him read of that scene on the sea, when the tempest-tossed soldiers and seamen, worn with labor and watching and long fasting, Paul the prisoner, on his way to trial and execution, spoke those grand words of courage and hope: "Be of good cheer: for there shall be no loss of any man's life among you. . . . For there stood by me this night the angel of God, whose I am, and whom I serve, saying, Fear not, Paul; thou must be brought before Caesar: and, lo, God hath given thee all them that sail with thee."

In the faith of this promise Paul assured his companions, "There shall not an hair fall from the head of any of you." So it came to pass. Because there was in that ship one man through whom God could work, the whole shipload of heathen soldiers and sailors was preserved. "They escaped all safe to land." Acts 27:22-24, 34, 44.

These things were not written merely that we might read and wonder, but that the same faith which wrought in God's servants of old might work in us. In no less marked a manner than He wrought then will He work now wherever there are hearts of faith to be channels of His power.

Let the self-distrustful, whose lack of self-reliance leads them to shrink from care and responsibility, be taught reliance upon God. Thus many a one who otherwise would be but a cipher in the world, perhaps only a helpless burden, will be able to say with the apostle Paul, "I can do all things through Christ which strengtheneth me." Philippians 4:13.

For the child also who is quick to resent injuries, faith has precious lessons. The disposition to resist evil or to avenge wrong is often prompted by a keen sense of justice and an active, energetic spirit. Let such a child be taught that God is the eternal guardian of right. He has a tender care for the beings whom He has so loved as to give His dearest Beloved to save. He will deal with every wrongdoer.

"For he that toucheth you toucheth the apple of His eye." Zechariah 2:8.

"Commit thy way unto the Lord; trust also in Him; and He shall bring it to pass. . . . He shall bring forth thy righteousness as the light, and thy judgment as the noonday." Psalm 37:5, 6.

"The Lord also will be a refuge for the oppressed, a refuge in times of trouble. And they that know Thy name will put their trust in Thee: for Thou, Lord, hast not forsaken them that seek Thee." Psalm 9:9, 10.

The compassion that God manifests toward us, He bids us manifest toward others. Let the impulsive, the self-sufficient, the revengeful, behold the meek and lowly One, let as a lamb to the slaughter, unretaliating as a sheep dumb before her shearers. Let them look upon Him whom our sins have pierced and our sorrows burdened, and they will learn to endure, to forbear, and to forgive.

Through faith in Christ, every deficiency of character may be supplied, every defilement cleansed, every fault corrected, every excellence developed.

"Ye are complete in Him." Colossians 2:10.

Prayer and faith are closely allied, and they need to be studied together. In the prayer of faith there is a divine science; it is a science that everyone who would make his lifework a success must understand. Christ says, "What things soever ye desire, when ye pray, believe that ye receive them, and ye shall have them." Mark 11:24. He makes it plain that our asking must be according to God's will; we must ask for the things that He has promised, and whatever we receive must be used in doing His will. The conditions met, the promise is unequivocal.

For the pardon of sin, for the Holy Spirit, for a Christlike temper, for wisdom and strength to do His work, for any gift He has promised, we may ask; then we are to believe that we receive, and return thanks to God that we have received.

We need look for no outward evidence of the blessing. The gift is in the promise, and we may go about our work assured that what God has promised He is able to perform, and that the gift, which we already possess, will be realized when we need it most.

To live thus by the word of God means the surrender to Him of the whole life. There will be felt a continual sense of need and dependence, a drawing out of the heart after God. Prayer is a necessity; for it is the life of the soul. Family prayer, public prayer, have their place; but it is secret communion with God that sustains the soul life.

It was in the mount with God that Moses beheld the pattern of that wonderful building which was to be the abiding place of His glory. It is in the mount with God—in the secret place of communion—that we are to contemplate His glorious ideal for humanity. Thus we shall be enabled so to fashion our character building that to us may be fulfilled His promise, "I will dwell in them, and walk in them; and I will be their God, and they shall be My people." 2 Corinthians 6:16.

It was in hours of solitary prayer that Jesus in His earth life received wisdom and power. Let the youth follow His example in finding at dawn and twilight a quiet season for communion with their Father in heaven. And throughout the day let them lift up their hearts to God. At every step of our way He says, "I the Lord thy God will hold thy right hand, . . . Fear not; I will help thee." Isaiah 41:13. Could our children learn these lessons in the morning of their years, what freshness and power, what joy and sweetness, would be brought into their lives!

These are lessons that only he who himself has learned can teach. It is because so many parents and teachers profess to believe the word of God while their lives deny its power, that the teaching of Scripture has no greater effect upon the youth. At times the youth are brought to feel the power of the word. They see the preciousness of the love of Christ. They see the beauty of His character, the possibilities of a life given to His service. But in contrast they see the life of those who profess to revere God's precepts. Of how many are the words true that were spoken to the prophet Ezekiel:

Thy people "speak one to another, everyone to his brother, saying, Come, I pray you, and hear what is the word that cometh forth from the Lord. And they come unto thee as the people cometh, and they sit before thee as My people, and they hear thy words, but they will not do them: for with their mouth they show much love, but their heart goeth after their covetousness. And, lo, thou art unto them as a very lovely song of one that hath a pleasant voice, and can play well on an instrument: for they hear thy words, but they do them not." Ezekiel 33:30-32.

It is one thing to treat the Bible as a book of good moral instruction, to be heeded so far as is consistent with the spirit of the times and our position in the world; it is another thing to regard it as it really is—the word of the living God, the word that is our life, the word that is to mold our actions, our words, and our thoughts. To hold God's word as anything less than this is to reject it. And this rejection by those who profess to believe it, is foremost among the causes of skepticism and infidelity in the youth.

An intensity such as never before was seen is taking possession of the world. In amusement, in moneymaking, in the contest for power, in the very struggle for existence, there is a terrible force that engrosses body and mind and soul. In the midst of this maddening rush, God is speaking. He bids us come apart and commune with Him. "Be still, and know that I am God." Psalm 46:10.

Many, even in their seasons of devotion, fail of receiving the blessing of real communion with God. They are in too great haste. With hurried steps they press through the circle of Christ's loving presence, pausing perhaps a moment within the sacred precincts, but not waiting for counsel. They have no time to remain with the divine Teacher. With their burdens they return to their work.

These workers can never attain the highest success until they learn the secret of strength. They must give themselves time to think, to pray, to wait upon God for a renewal of physical, mental, and spiritual power. They need the uplifting influence of His Spirit. Receiving this, they will be quickened by fresh life. The wearied frame and tired brain will be refreshed, the burdened heart will be lightened.

Not a pause for a moment in His presence, but personal contact with Christ, to sit down in companionship with Him—this is our need. Happy will it be for the children of our homes and the students of our schools when parents and teachers shall learn in their own lives the precious experience pictured in these words from the Song of Songs:

> "As the apple tree among the trees of the wood,
> So is my Beloved among the sons.
> I sat down under His shadow with great delight,
> And His fruit was sweet to my taste.
> He brought me to the banqueting house,
> And His banner over me was love."
>
> Song of Solomon 2:3, 4.

31
The Lifework

"This one thing I do."

Success in any line demands a definite aim. He who would achieve true success in life must keep steadily in view the aim worthy of his endeavor. Such an aim is set before the youth of today. The heaven-appointed purpose of giving the gospel to the world in this generation is the noblest that can appeal to any human being. It opens a field of effort to everyone whose heart Christ has touched.

God's purpose for the children growing up beside our hearths is wider, deeper, higher, than our restricted vision has comprehended. From the humblest lot those whom He has seen faithful have in time past been called to witness for Him in the world's highest places. And many a lad of today, growing up as did Daniel in his Judean home, studying God's word and His works, and learning the lessons of faithful service, will yet stand in legislative assemblies, in halls of justice, or in royal courts, as a witness for the King of kings. Multitudes will be called to a wider ministry. The whole world is opening to the gospel. Ethiopia is stretching out her hands unto God. From Japan and China and India, from the still-darkened lands of our own continent, from every quarter of this world of ours, comes the cry of sin-stricken hearts for a knowledge of the God of love. Millions upon millions have never so much as heard of God or of His love revealed in Christ. It is their right to receive this knowledge. They have an equal claim with us in the Saviour's mercy. And it rests with us who have received the knowledge, with our children to whom we may impart it, to answer their cry. To every household and every school, to every parent, teacher, and child upon whom has shone the light of the gospel, comes at this crisis the question put to Esther the queen at that momentous crisis in Israel's history, "Who knoweth whether *thou* art come to the kingdom for such a time as this?" Esther 4:14.

Those who think of the result of hastening or hindering the gospel think of it in relation to themselves and to the world. Few think of its relation to God. Few give thought to the suffering that sin has caused our Creator. All heaven suffered in Christ's agony; but that suffering did not begin or end with His manifestation in humanity. The cross is a revelation to our dull senses of the pain that, from its very inception, sin has brought to the heart of God. Every departure from the right, every deed of cruelty, every failure of humanity to reach His ideal, brings grief to Him. When there came upon Israel the calamities that were the sure result of separation from God—subjugation by their enemies, cruelty, and death—it is said that "His soul was grieved for the misery of Israel." "In all their affliction He was afflicted: . . . and He bare them, and carried them all the days of old." Judges 10:16; Isaiah 63:9.

His Spirit "maketh intercession for us with groanings which cannot be uttered." As the "whole creation groaneth and travaileth in pain together" (Romans 8:26, 22), the heart of the infinite Father is pained in sympathy. Our world is a vast lazar house, a scene of misery that we dare not allow even our thoughts to dwell upon. Did we realize it as it is, the burden would be too terrible. Yet God feels it all. In order to destroy sin and its results He gave His best Beloved, and He has put it in our power, through co-operation with Him, to bring this scene of misery to an end. "This gospel of the kingdom shall be preached in all the world for a witness unto all nations; and then shall the end come." Matthew 24:14.

"Go ye into all the world, and preach the gospel to every creature" (Mark 16:15), is Christ's command to His followers. Not that all are called to be ministers or missionaries in the ordinary sense of the term; but all may be workers with Him in giving the "glad tidings" to their fellow men. To all, great or small, learned or ignorant, old or young, the command is given.

In view of this command, can we educate our sons and daughters for a life of respectable conventionality, a life professedly Christian, but lacking His self-sacrifice, a life on which the verdict of Him who is truth must be, "I know you not"?

Thousands are doing this. They think to secure for their children the benefits of the gospel while they deny its spirit. But this cannot be. Those who reject the privilege of fellowship with Christ in service, reject the only training that imparts a fitness for participation with Him in His glory. They reject the training that in this life gives strength and nobility of character. Many a father and mother, denying their children to the cross of Christ, have learned too late that they were thus giving them over to the enemy of God and man. They sealed their ruin, not alone for the future but for the present life. Temptation overcame them. They grew up a curse to the world, a grief and shame to those who gave them being.

Even in seeking a preparation for God's service, many are turned aside by wrong methods of education. Life is too generally regarded as made up of distinct periods, the period of learning and the period of doing—of preparation and of achievement. In preparation for a life of service the youth are sent to school, to acquire knowledge by the study of books. Cut off from the responsibilities of everyday life, they become absorbed in study, and often lose sight of its purpose. The ardor of their early consecration dies out, and too many take up with some personal, selfish ambition. Upon their graduation, thousands find themselves out of touch with life. They have so long dealt with the abstract and theoretical that when the whole being must be roused to meet the sharp contests of real life, they are unprepared. Instead of the noble work they had purposed, their energies are engrossed in a struggle for mere subsistence. After repeated disappointments, in despair even of earning an honest livelihood, many drift into questionable or criminal practices. The world is robbed of the service it might have received; and God is robbed of the souls He longed to uplift, ennoble, and honor as representatives of Himself.

Many parents err in discriminating between their children in the matter of education. They make almost any sacrifice to secure the best advantages for one that is bright and apt. But these opportunities are not thought a necessity for those who are less promising. Little education is deemed essential for the performance of life's ordinary duties.

But who is capable of selecting from a family of children the ones upon whom will rest the most important responsibilities? How often human judgment has here proved to be at fault! Remember the experience of Samuel when sent to anoint from the sons of Jesse one to be king over Israel. Seven noble-looking youth passed before him. As he looked upon the first, in features comely, in form well-developed, and in bearing princely, the prophet exclaimed, "Surely the Lord's anointed is before Him." But God said, "Look not on his countenance, or on the height of his stature; because I have refused him: for the Lord seeth not as man seeth; for man looketh on the outward appearance, but the Lord looketh on the heart." So of all the seven the testimony was, "The Lord hath not chosen these." 1 Samuel 16:6, 7, 10. And not until David had been called from the flock was the prophet permitted to fulfill his mission.

The elder brothers, from whom Samuel would have chosen, did not possess the qualifications that God saw to be essential in a ruler of His people. Proud, self-centered, self-confident, they were set aside for the one whom they lightly regarded, one who had preserved the simplicity and sincerity of his youth, and who, while little in his own sight, could be trained by God for the responsibilities of the kingdom. So today, in many a child whom the parents would pass by, God sees capabilities far above those revealed by others who are thought to possess great promise.

And as regards life's possibilities, who is capable of deciding what is great and what is small? How many a worker in the lowly places of life, by setting on foot agencies for the blessing of the world, has achieved results that kings might envy!

Let every child, then, receive an education for the highest service. "In the morning sow thy seed, and in the evening withhold not thine hand: for thou knowest not which shall prosper, whether this or that," Ecclesiastes 11:6, R.V.

The specific place appointed us in life is determined by our capabilities.

Not all reach the same development or do with equal efficiency the same work. God does not expect the hyssop to attain the proportions of the cedar, or the olive the height of the stately palm. But each should aim just as high as the union of human with divine power makes it possible for him to reach.

Many do not become what they might, because they do not put forth the power that is in them. They do not, as they might, lay hold on divine strength. Many are diverted from the line in which they might reach the truest success. Seeking greater honor or a more pleasing task, they attempt something for which they are not fitted. Many a man whose talents are adapted for some other calling, is ambitious to enter a profession; and he who might have been successful as a farmer, an artisan, or a nurse, fills inadequately the position of a minister, a lawyer, or a physician. There are others, again, who might have filled a responsible calling, but who, for want of energy, application, or perseverance, content themselves with an easier place.

We need to follow more closely God's plan of life. To do our best in the work that lies nearest, to commit our ways to God, and to watch for the indications of His providence—these are rules that ensure safe guidance in the choice of an occupation.

He who came from heaven to be our example spent nearly thirty years of His life in common, mechanical labor; but during this time He was studying the word and the works of God, and helping, teaching, all whom His influence could reach. When His public ministry began, He went about healing the sick, comforting the sorrowful, and preaching the gospel to the poor. This is the work of all His followers.

"He that is greatest among you," He said, "let him be as the younger; and he that is chief, as he that doth serve. For . . . I am among you as he that serveth." Luke 22:26, 27.

Love and loyalty to Christ are the spring of all true service. In the heart touched by His love, there is begotten a desire to work for Him. Let this desire be encouraged and rightly guided. Whether in the home, the neighborhood, or the school, the presence of the poor, the afflicted, the ignorant, or the unfortunate should be regarded, not as a misfortune, but as affording precious opportunity for service.

In this work, as in every other, skill is gained in the work itself. It is by training in the common duties of life and in ministry to the needy and suffering, that efficiency is assured. Without this the best-meant efforts are often useless and even harmful. It is in the water, not on the land, that men learn to swim.

Another obligation, too often lightly regarded—one that to the youth awakened to the claims of Christ needs to be made plain—is the obligation of church relationship.

Very close and sacred is the relation between Christ and His church—He the bridegroom, and the church the bride; He the head, and the church the body. Connection with Christ, then, involves connection with His church.

The church is organized for service; and in a life of service to Christ, connection with the church is one of the first steps. Loyalty to Christ demands the faithful performance of church duties. This is an important part of one's training; and in a church imbued with the Master's life, it will lead directly to effort for the world without.

There are many lines in which the youth can find opportunity for helpful effort. Let them organize into bands for Christian service, and the co-operation will prove an assistance and an encouragement. Parents and teachers, by taking an interest in the work of the young people, will be able to give them the benefit of their own larger experience, and can help them to make their efforts effective for good.

It is acquaintance that awakens sympathy, and sympathy is the spring of effective ministry. To awaken in the children and youth sympathy and the spirit of sacrifice for the suffering millions in the "regions beyond," let them become acquainted with these lands and their peoples. In this line much might be accomplished in our schools. Instead of dwelling on the exploits of the Alexanders and Napoleons of history, let the pupils study the lives of such men as the apostle Paul and Martin Luther, as Moffat and Livingstone and Carey, and the present daily-unfolding history of missionary effort. Instead of burdening their memories with an array of names and theories that have no bearing upon their lives, and to which, once outside the schoolroom, they rarely give a thought, let them study all lands in the light of missionary effort and become acquainted with the peoples and their needs.

In this closing work of the gospel there is a vast field to be occupied; and, more than ever before, the work is to enlist helpers from the common people. Both the youth and those older in years will be called from the field, from the vineyard, and from the workshop, and sent forth by the Master to give His message. Many of these have had little opportunity for education; but Christ sees in them qualifications that will enable them to fulfill His purpose. If they put their hearts into the work, and continue to be learners, He will fit them to labor for Him.

He who knows the depths of the world's misery and despair, knows by what means to bring relief. He sees on every hand souls in darkness, bowed down with sin and sorrow and pain. But He sees also their possibilities; He sees the height to which they may attain. Although human beings have abused their mercies, wasted their talents, and lost the dignity of godlike manhood, the Creator is to be glorified in their redemption.

The burden of labor for these needy ones in the rough places of the earth Christ lays upon those who can feel for the ignorant and for such as are out of the way. He will be present to help those whose hearts are susceptible to pity, though their hands may be rough and unskilled. He will work through those who can see mercy in misery, and gain in loss. When the Light of the world passes by, privilege will be discerned in hardship, order in confusion, success in apparent failure. Calamities will be seen as disguised blessings; woes, as mercies. Laborers from the common people, sharing the sorrows of their fellow men as their Master shared the sorrows of the whole human race, will by faith see Him working with them.

"The great day of the Lord is near, it is near, and hasteth greatly." Zephaniah 1:14. And a world is to be warned.

With such preparation as they can gain, thousands upon thousands of the youth and those older in years should be giving themselves to this work. Already many hearts are responding to the call of the Master Worker, and their numbers will increase. Let every Christian educator give such workers sympathy and co-operation. Let him encourage and assist the youth under his care in gaining a preparation to join the ranks.

There is no line of work in which it is possible for the youth to receive greater benefit. All who engage in ministry are God's helping hand. They are co-workers with the angels; rather, they are the human agencies through whom the angels accomplish their mission. Angels speak through their voices, and work by their hands. And the human workers, co-operating with heavenly agencies, have the benefit of their education and experience. As a means of education, what "university course" can equal this?

With such an army of workers as our youth, rightly trained, might furnish, how soon the message of a crucified, risen, and soon-coming Saviour might be carried to the whole world! How soon might the end come—the end of suffering and sorrow and sin! How soon, in place of a possession here, with its blight of sin and pain, our children might receive their inheritance where "the righteous shall inherit the land, and dwell therein forever;" where "the inhabitant shall not say, I am sick," and "the voice of weeping shall be no more heard." Psalm 37:29; Isaiah 33:24; 65:19.

The Underteacher

"As My Father hath sent Me, even so send I you."

32
Preparation

"Study to show thyself approved unto God."

The child's first teacher is the mother. During the period of greatest susceptibility and most rapid development his education is to a great degree in her hands. To her first is given opportunity to mold the character for good or for evil. She should understand the value of her opportunity, and, above every other teacher, should be qualified to use it to the best account. Yet there is no other to whose training so little thought is given. The one whose influence in education is most potent and far-reaching is the one for whose assistance there is the least systematic effort.

Those to whom the care of the little child is committed are too often ignorant of its physical needs; they know little of the laws of health or the principles of development. Nor are they better fitted to care for its mental and spiritual growth. They may be qualified to conduct business or to shine in society; they may have made creditable attainments in literature and science; but of the training of a child they have little knowledge. It is chiefly because of this lack, especially because of the early neglect of physical development, that so large a proportion of the human race die in infancy, and of those who reach maturity there are so many to whom life is but a burden.

Upon fathers as well as mothers rests a responsibility for the child's earlier as well as its later training, and for both parents the demand for careful and thorough preparation is most urgent. Before taking upon themselves the possibilities of fatherhood and motherhood, men and women should become acquainted with the laws of physical development—with physiology and hygiene, with the bearing of prenatal influences, with the laws of heredity, sanitation, dress, exercise, and the treatment of disease; they should also understand the laws of mental development and moral training.

This work of education the Infinite One has counted so important that messengers from His throne have been sent to a mother that was to be, to answer the question, "How shall we order the child, and how shall we do unto him?" (Judges 13:12), and to instruct a father concerning the education of a promised son.

Never will education accomplish all that it might and should accomplish until the importance of the parents' work is fully recognized, and they receive a training for its sacred responsibilities.

The necessity of preparatory training for the teacher is universally admitted; but few recognize the character of the preparation most essential. He who appreciates the responsibility involved in the training of the youth, will realize that instruction in scientific and literary lines alone cannot suffice. The teacher should have a more comprehensive education than can be gained by the study of books. He should possess not only strength but breadth of mind; should be not only whole-souled but large-hearted.

He only who created the mind and ordained its laws can perfectly understand its needs or direct its development. The principles of education that He has given are the only safe guide. A qualification essential for every teacher is a knowledge of these principles and such an acceptance of them as will make them a controlling power in his own life.

Experience in practical life is indispensable. Order, thoroughness, punctuality, self-control, a sunny temper, evenness of disposition, self-sacrifice, integrity, and courtesy are essential qualifications.

Because there is so much cheapness of character, so much of the counterfeit all around the youth, there is the more need that the teacher's words, attitude, and deportment should represent the elevated and the true. Children are quick to detect affectation or any other weakness or defect. The teacher can gain the respect of his pupils in no other way than by revealing in his own character the principles which he seeks to teach them. Only as he does this in his daily association with them can he have a permanent influence over them for good.

For almost every other qualification that contributes to his success, the teacher is in great degree dependent upon physical vigor. The better his health, the better will be his work.

So wearing are his responsibilities that special effort on his part is required to preserve vigor and freshness. Often he becomes heart-weary and brain-weary, with the almost irresistible tendency to depression, coldness, or irritability. It is his duty not merely to resist such moods but to avoid their cause. He needs to keep the heart pure and sweet and trustful and sympathetic. In order to be always firm and calm and cheerful, he must preserve the strength of brain and nerve.

Since in his work quality is so much more important than quantity, he should guard against overlabor—against attempting too much in his own line of duty; against accepting other responsibilities that would unfit him for his work; and against engaging in amusements and social pleasures that are exhausting rather than recuperative.

Outdoor exercise, especially in useful labor, is one of the best means of recreation for body and mind; and the teacher's example will inspire his pupils with interest in, and respect for, manual labor.

In every line the teacher should scrupulously observe the principles of health. He should do this not only because of its bearing upon his own usefulness, but also because of its influence upon his pupils. He should be temperate in all things; in diet, dress, labor, recreation, he is to be an example.

With physical health and uprightness of character should be combined high literary qualifications. The more of true knowledge the teacher has, the better will be his work. The schoolroom is no place for surface work. No teacher who is satisfied with superficial knowledge will attain a high degree of efficiency.

But the teacher's usefulness depends not so much upon the actual amount of his acquirements as upon the standard at which he aims. The true teacher is not content with dull thoughts, an indolent mind, or a loose memory. He constantly seeks higher attainments and better methods. His life is one of continual growth. In the work of such a teacher there is a freshness, a quickening power, that awakens and inspires his pupils.

The teacher must have aptness for his work. He must have the wisdom and tact required in dealing with minds. However great his scientific knowledge, however excellent his qualifications in other lines, if he does not gain the respect and confidence of his pupils, his efforts will be in vain.

Teachers are needed who are quick to discern and improve every opportunity for doing good; those who with enthusiasm combine true dignity, who are able to control, and "apt to teach," who can inspire thought, arouse energy, and impart courage and life.

A teacher's advantages may have been limited, so that he may not possess as high literary qualifications as might be desirable; yet if he has true insight into human nature; if he has a genuine love for his work, an appreciation of its magnitude, and a determination to improve; if he is willing to labor earnestly and perseveringly, he will comprehend the needs of his pupils, and, by his sympathetic, progressive spirit, will inspire them to follow as he seeks to lead them onward and upward.

The children and youth under the teacher's care differ widely in disposition, habits, and training. Some have no definite purpose or fixed principles. They need to be awakened to their responsibilities and possibilities. Few children have been rightly trained at home. Some have been household pets. Their whole training has been superficial. Allowed to follow inclination and to shun responsibility and burden bearing, they lack stability, perseverance, and self-denial. These often regard all discipline as an unnecessary restraint. Others have been censured and discouraged. Arbitrary restraint and harshness have developed in them obstinacy and defiance. If these deformed characters are reshaped, the work must, in most cases, be done by the teacher. In order to accomplish it successfully, he must have the sympathy and insight that will enable him to trace to their cause the faults and errors manifest in his pupils. He must have also the tact and skill, the patience and firmness, that will enable him to impart to each the needed help—to the vacillating and ease loving, such encouragement and assistance as will be a stimulus to exertion; to the discouraged, sympathy and appreciation that will create confidence and thus inspire effort.

Teachers often fail of coming sufficiently into social relation with their pupils. They manifest too little sympathy and tenderness, and too much of the dignity of the stern judge. While the teacher must be firm and decided, he should not be exacting or dictatorial. To be harsh and censorious, to stand aloof from his pupils or treat them indifferently, is to close the avenues through which he might influence them for good.

Under no circumstances should the teacher manifest partiality. To favor the winning, attractive pupil, and be critical, impatient, or unsympathetic toward those who most need encouragement and help, is to reveal a total misconception of the teacher's work. It is in dealing with the faulty, trying ones that the character is tested, and it is proved whether the teacher is really qualified for his position.

Great is the responsibility of those who take upon themselves the guidance of a human soul. The true father and mother count theirs a trust from which they can never be wholly released. The life of the child, from his earliest to his latest day, feels the power of that tie which binds him to the parent's heart; the acts, the words, the very look of the parent, continue to mold the child for good or for evil. The teacher shares this responsibility, and he needs constantly to realize its sacredness, and to keep in view the purpose of his work. He is not merely to accomplish the daily tasks, to please his employers, to maintain the standing of the school; he must consider the highest good of his pupils as individuals, the duties that life will lay upon them, the service it requires, and the preparation demanded. The work he is doing day by day will exert upon his pupils, and through them upon others, an influence that will not cease to extend and strengthen until time shall end. The fruits of his work he must meet in that great day when every word and deed shall be brought in review before God.

The teacher who realizes this will not feel that his work is completed when he has finished the daily routine of recitations, and for a time his pupils pass from under his direct care. He will carry these children and youth upon his heart. How to secure for them the noblest standard of attainment will be his constant study and effort.

He who discerns the opportunities and privileges of his work will allow nothing to stand in the way of earnest endeavor for self-improvement. He will spare no pains to reach the highest standard of excellence. All that he desires his pupils to become, he will himself strive to be.

The deeper the sense of responsibility, and the more earnest the effort for self-improvement, the more clearly will the teacher perceive and the more keenly regret the defects that hinder his usefulness. As he beholds the magnitude of his work, its difficulties and possibilities, often will his heart cry out, "Who is sufficient for these things?"

Dear teacher, as you consider your need of strength and guidance—need that no human source can supply—I bid you consider the promises of Him who is the wonderful Counselor.

"Behold," He says, "I have set before thee an open door, and no man can shut it." Revelation 3:8.

"Call unto Me, and I will answer thee." "I will instruct thee and teach thee in the way which thou shalt go: I will guide thee with Mine eye." Jeremiah 33:3; Psalm 32:8.

"Even unto the end of the world" "I am with you." Matthew 28:20.

As the highest preparation for your work, I point you to the words, the life, the methods, of the Prince of teachers. I bid you consider Him. Here is your true ideal. Behold it, dwell upon it, until the Spirit of the divine Teacher shall take possession of your heart and life.

"Reflecting as a mirror the glory of the Lord," you will be "transformed into the same image." 2 Corinthians 3:18, R.V.

This is the secret of power over your pupils. Reflect Him.

33
Co-operation

"We are members one of another."

In the formation of character, no other influences count so much as the influence of the home. The teacher's work should supplement that of the parents, but is not to take its place. In all that concerns the well-being of the child, it should be the effort of parents and teachers to co-operate.

The work of co-operation should begin with the father and mother themselves, in the home life. In the training of their children they have a joint responsibility, and it should be their constant endeavor to act together. Let them yield themselves to God, seeking help from Him to sustain each other. Let them teach their children to be true to God, true to principle, and thus true to themselves and to all with whom they are connected. With such training, children when sent to school will not be a cause of disturbance or anxiety. They will be a support to their teachers, and an example and encouragement to their fellow pupils.

Parents who give this training are not the ones likely to be found criticizing the teacher. They feel that both the interest of their children and justice to the school demand that, so far as possible, they sustain and honor the one who shares their responsibility.

Many parents fail here. By their hasty, unfounded criticism the influence of the faithful, self-sacrificing teacher is often well-nigh destroyed. Many parents whose children have been spoiled by indulgence, leave to the teacher the unpleasant task of repairing their neglect; and then by their own course they make his task almost hopeless. Their criticism and censure of the school management encourage insubordination in the children, and confirm them in wrong habits.

If criticism or suggestion in regard to the teacher's work becomes necessary, it should be made to him in private. If this proves ineffective, let the matter be referred to those who are responsible for the management of the school. Nothing should be said or done to weaken the children's respect for the one upon whom their well-being in so great degree depends.

The parents' intimate knowledge both of the character of the children and of their physical peculiarities or infirmities, if imparted to the teacher, would be an assistance to him. It is to be regretted that so many fail of realizing this. By most parents little interest is shown either to inform themselves as to the teacher's qualifications, or to co-operate with him in his work.

Since parents so rarely acquaint themselves with the teacher, it is the more important that the teacher seek the acquaintance of parents. He should visit the homes of his pupils and gain a knowledge of the influences and surroundings among which they live. By coming personally in touch with their homes and lives, he may strengthen the ties that bind him to his pupils and may learn how to deal more successfully with their different dispositions and temperaments.

As he interests himself in the home education, the teacher imparts a double benefit. Many parents, absorbed in work and care, lose sight of their opportunities to influence for good the lives of their children. The teacher can do much to arouse these parents to their possibilities and privileges. He will find others to whom the sense of their responsibility is a heavy burden, so anxious are they that their children shall become good and useful men and women. Often the teacher can assist these parents in bearing their burden, and, by counseling together, both teacher and parents will be encouraged and strengthened.

In the home training of the youth the principle of co-operation is invaluable. From their earliest years children should be led to feel that they are a part of the home firm. Even the little ones should be trained to share in the daily work and should be made to feel that their help is needed and is appreciated. The older ones should be their parents' assistants, entering into their plans and sharing their responsibilities and burdens. Let fathers and mothers take time to teach their children, let them show that they value their help, desire their confidence, and enjoy their companionship, and the children will not be slow to respond. Not only will the parents' burden be lightened, and the children receive a practical training of inestimable worth, but there will be a strengthening of the home ties and a deepening of the very foundations of character.

Co-operation should be the spirit of the schoolroom, the law of its life. The teacher who gains the co-operation of his pupils secures an invaluable aid in maintaining order. In service in the schoolroom many a boy whose restlessness leads to disorder and insubordination would find an outlet for his superfluous energy. Let the older assist the younger, the strong the weak; and, so far as possible, let each be called upon to do something in which he excels. This will encourage self-respect and a desire to be useful.

It would be helpful for the youth, and for parents and teachers as well, to study the lesson of co-operation as taught in the Scriptures. Among its many illustrations notice the building of the tabernacle—that object lesson of character building—in which the whole people united, "everyone whose heart stirred him up, and everyone whom his spirit made willing." Exodus 35:21. Read how the wall of Jerusalem was rebuilt by the returned captives, in the midst of poverty, difficulty, and danger, the great task successfully accomplished because "the people had a mind to work." Nehemiah 4:6. Consider the part acted by the disciples in the Saviour's miracle for the feeding of the multitude. The food multiplied in the hands of Christ, but the disciples received the loaves and gave to the waiting throng.

"We are members one of another." As everyone therefore "hath received a (R.V.) gift, even so minister the same one to another, as good stewards of the manifold grace of God." Ephesians 4:25; 1 Peter 4:10.

Well might the words written of the idol builders of old be, with worthier aim, adopted as a motto by character builders of today:

"They helped everyone his neighbor; and everyone said to his brother, Be of good courage." Isaiah 41:6.

34
Discipline

"Train, admonish, encourage, be long-suffering."

One of the first lessons a child needs to learn is the lesson of obedience. Before he is old enough to reason, he may be taught to obey. By gentle, persistent effort, the habit should be established. Thus, to a great degree, may be prevented those later conflicts between will and authority that do so much to create alienation and bitterness toward parents and teachers, and too often resistance of all authority, human and divine.

The object of discipline is the training of the child for self-government. He should be taught self-reliance and self-control. Therefore as soon as he is capable of understanding, his reason should be enlisted on the side of obedience. Let all dealing with him be such as to show obedience to be just and reasonable. Help him to see that all things are under law, and that disobedience leads, in the end, to disaster and suffering. When God says "Thou shalt not," He in love warns us of the consequences of disobedience, in order to save us from harm and loss.

Help the child to see that parents and teachers are representatives of God, and that, as they act in harmony with Him, their laws in the home and the school are also His. As the child is to render obedience to parents and teachers, so they, in turn, are to render obedience to God.

To direct the child's development without hindering it by undue control should be the study of both parent and teacher. Too much management is as bad as too little. The effort to "break the will" of a child is a terrible mistake. Minds are constituted differently; while force may secure outward submission, the result with many children is a more determined rebellion of the heart. Even should the parent or teacher succeed in gaining the control he seeks, the outcome may be no less harmful to the child. The discipline of a human being who has reached the years of intelligence should differ from the training of a dumb animal. The beast is taught only submission to its master. For the beast, the master is mind, judgment, and will. This method, sometimes employed in the training of children, makes them little more than automatons. Mind, will, conscience, are under the control of another. It is not God's purpose that any mind should be thus dominated. Those who weaken or destroy individuality assume a responsibility that can result only in evil. While under authority, the children may appear like well-drilled soldiers; but when the control ceases, the character will be found to lack strength and steadfastness. Having never learned to govern himself, the youth recognizes no restraint except the requirement of parents or teacher. This removed, he knows not how to use his liberty, and often gives himself up to indulgence that proves his ruin.

Since the surrender of the will is so much more difficult for some pupils than for others, the teacher should make obedience to his requirements as easy as possible. The will should be guided and molded, but not ignored or crushed. Save the strength of the will; in the battle of life it will be needed.

Every child should understand the true force of the will. He should be led to see how great is the responsibility involved in this gift. The will is the governing power in the nature of man, the power of decision, or choice. Every human being possessed of reason has power to choose the right. In every experience of life, God's word to us is, "Choose you this day whom ye will serve." Joshua 24:15. Everyone may place his will on the side of the will of God, may choose to obey Him, and by thus linking himself with divine agencies, he may stand where nothing can force him to do evil. In every youth, every child, lies the power, by the help of God, to form a character of integrity and to live a life of usefulness.

The parent or teacher who by such instruction trains the child to self-control will be the most useful and permanently successful. To the superficial observer his work may not appear to the best advantage; it may not be valued so highly as that of the one who holds the mind and will of the child under absolute authority; but after years will show the result of the better method of training.

The wise educator, in dealing with his pupils, will seek to encourage confidence and to strengthen the sense of honor. Children and youth are benefited by being trusted. Many, even of the little children, have a high sense of honor; all desire to be treated with confidence and respect, and this is their right. They should not be led to feel that they cannot go out or come in without being watched. Suspicion demoralizes, producing the very evils it seeks to prevent. Instead of watching continually, as if suspecting evil, teachers who are in touch with their pupils will discern the workings of the restless mind, and will set to work influences that will counteract evil. Lead the youth to feel that they are trusted, and there are few who will not seek to prove themselves worthy of the trust.

On the same principle it is better to request than to command; the one thus addressed has opportunity to prove himself loyal to right principles. His obedience is the result of choice rather than compulsion.

The rules governing the schoolroom should, so far as possible, represent the voice of the school. Every principle involved in them should be so placed before the student that he may be convinced of its justice. Thus he will feel a responsibility to see that the rules which he himself has helped to frame are obeyed.

Rules should be few and well considered; and when once made, they should be enforced. Whatever it is found impossible to change, the mind learns to recognize and adapt itself to; but the possibility of indulgence induces desire, hope, and uncertainty, and the results are restlessness, irritably, and insubordination.

It should be made plain that the government of God knows no compromise with evil. Neither in the home nor in the school should disobedience be tolerated. No parent or teacher who has at heart the well-being of those under his care will compromise with the stubborn self-will that defies authority or resorts to subterfuge or evasion in order to escape obedience. It is not love but sentimentalism that palters with wrongdoing, seeks by coaxing or bribes to secure compliance, and finally accepts some substitute in place of the thing required.

"Fools make a mock at sin." Proverbs 14:9. We should beware of treating sin as a light thing. Terrible is its power over the wrongdoer. "His own iniquities shall take the wicked himself, and he shall be holden with the cords of his sins." Proverbs 5:22. The greatest wrong done to a child or youth is to allow him to become fastened in the bondage of evil habit.

The youth have an inborn love of liberty; they desire freedom; and they need to understand that these inestimable blessings are to be enjoyed only in obedience to the law of God. This law is the preserver of true freedom and liberty. It points out and prohibits those things that degrade and enslave, and thus to the obedient it affords protection from the power of evil.

The psalmist says: "I will walk at liberty: for I seek Thy precepts." "Thy testimonies also are my delight and my counselors." Psalm 119:45, 24.

In our efforts to correct evil, we should guard against a tendency to faultfinding or censure. Continual censure bewilders, but does not reform. With many minds, and often those of the finest susceptibility, an atmosphere of unsympathetic criticism is fatal to effort. Flowers do not unfold under the breath of a blighting wind.

A child frequently censured for some special fault, comes to regard that fault as his peculiarity, something against which it is vain to strive. Thus are created discouragement and hopelessness, often concealed under an appearance of indifference or bravado.

The true object of reproof is gained only when the wrongdoer himself is led to see his fault and his will is enlisted for its correction. When this is accomplished, point him to the source of pardon and power. Seek to preserve his self-respect and to inspire him with courage and hope.

This work is the nicest, the most difficult, ever committed to human beings. It requires the most delicate tact, the finest susceptibility, a knowledge of human nature, and a heaven-born faith and patience, willing to work and watch and wait. It is a work than which nothing can be more important.

Those who desire to control others must first control themselves. To deal passionately with a child or youth will only arouse his resentment. When a parent or teacher becomes impatient and is in danger of speaking unwisely, let him remain silent. There is wonderful power in silence.

The teacher must expect to meet perverse dispositions and obdurate hearts. But in dealing with them he should never forget that he himself was once a child, in need of discipline. Even now, with all his advantages of age, education, and experience, he often errs, and is in need of mercy and forbearance. In training the youth he should consider that he is dealing with those who have inclinations to evil similar to his own. They have almost everything to learn, and it is much more difficult for some to learn than for others. With the dull pupil he should bear patiently, not censuring his ignorance, but improving every opportunity to give him encouragement. With sensitive, nervous pupils he should deal very tenderly. A sense of his own imperfections should lead him constantly to manifest sympathy and forbearance toward those who also are struggling with difficulties.

The Saviour's rule—"As ye would that men should do to you, do ye also to them likewise" (Luke 6:31)—should be the rule of all who undertake the training of children and youth. They are the younger members of the Lord's family, heirs with us of the grace of life. Christ's rule should be sacredly observed toward the dullest, the youngest, the most blundering, and even toward the erring and rebellious.

This rule will lead the teacher to avoid, so far as possible, making public the faults or errors of a pupil. He will seek to avoid giving reproof or punishment in the presence of others. He will not expel a student until every effort has been put forth for his reformation. But when it becomes evident that the student is receiving no benefit himself, while his defiance or disregard of authority tends to overthrow the government of the school, and his influence is contaminating others, then his expulsion becomes a necessity. Yet with many the disgrace of public expulsion would lead to utter recklessness and ruin. In most cases when removal is unavoidable, the matter need not be made public. By counsel and co-operation with the parents, let the teacher privately arrange for the student's withdrawal.

In this time of special danger for the young, temptations surround them on every hand; and while it is easy to drift, the strongest effort is required in order to press against the current. Every school should be a "city of refuge" for the tempted youth, a place where their follies shall be dealt with patiently and wisely. Teachers who understand their responsibilities will separate from their own hearts and lives everything that would prevent them from dealing successfully with the willful and disobedient. Love and tenderness, patience and self-control, will at all times be the law of their speech. Mercy and compassion will be blended with justice. When it is necessary to give reproof, their language will not be exaggerated, but humble. In gentleness they will set before the wrongdoer his errors and help him to recover himself. Every true teacher will feel that should he err at all, it is better to err on the side of mercy than on the side of severity.

Many youth who are thought incorrigible are not at heart so hard as they appear. Many who are regarded as hopeless may be reclaimed by wise discipline. These are often the ones who most readily melt under kindness. Let the teacher gain the confidence of the tempted one, and by recognizing and developing the good in his character, he can, in many cases, correct the evil without calling attention to it.

The divine Teacher bears with the erring through all their perversity. His love does not grow cold; His efforts to win them do not cease. With outstretched arms He waits to welcome again and again the erring, the rebellious, and even the apostate. His heart is touched with the helplessness of the little child subject to rough usage. The cry of human suffering never reaches His ear in vain. Though all are precious in His sight, the rough, sullen, stubborn dispositions draw most heavily upon His sympathy and love; for He traces from cause to effect. The one who is most easily tempted, and is most inclined to err, is the special object of His solicitude.

Every parent and every teacher should cherish the attributes of Him who makes the cause of the afflicted, the suffering, and the tempted His own. He should be one who can have "compassion on the ignorant, and on them that are out of the way; for that he himself also is compassed with infirmity." Hebrews 5:2. Jesus treats us far better than we deserve; and as He has treated us, so we are to treat others. The course of no parent or teacher is justifiable if it is unlike that which under similar circumstances the Saviour would pursue.

Meeting Life's Discipline

Beyond the discipline of the home and the school, all have to meet the stern discipline of life. How to meet this wisely is a lesson that should be made plain to every child and to every youth. It is true that God loves us, that He is working for our happiness, and that, if His law had always been obeyed, we should never have known suffering; and it is no less true that, in this world, as the result of sin, suffering, trouble, burdens, come to every life. We may do the children and the youth a lifelong good by teaching them to meet bravely these troubles and burdens. While we should give them sympathy, let it never be such as to foster self-pity. What they need is that which stimulates and strengthens rather than weakens.

They should be taught that this world is not a parade ground, but a battlefield. All are called to endure hardness, as good soldiers. They are to be strong and quit themselves like men. Let them be taught that the true test of character is found in the willingness to bear burdens, to take the hard place, to do the work that needs to be done, though it bring no earthly recognition or reward.

The true way of dealing with trial is not by seeking to escape it, but by transforming it. This applies to all discipline, the earlier as well as the later. The neglect of the child's earliest training, and the consequent strengthening of wrong tendencies, makes his after education more difficult, and causes discipline to be too often a painful process. Painful it must be to the lower nature, crossing, as it does, the natural desires and inclinations; but the pain may be lost sight of in a higher joy.

Let the child and the youth be taught that every mistake, every fault, every difficulty, conquered, becomes a stepping-stone to better and higher things. It is through such experiences that all who have ever made life worth the living have achieved success.

"The heights by great men reached and kept
Were not attained by sudden flight,
But they, while their companions slept,
Were toiling upward in the night."

"We rise by things that are under our feet;
By what we have mastered of good and gain;
By the pride deposed and the passion slain,
And the vanquished ills that we hourly meet."

"All common things, each day's events,
That with the hour begin and end,
Our pleasures and our discontents,
Are rounds by which we may ascend."

We are to "look not at the things which are seen, but at the things which are not seen: for the things which are seen are temporal; but the things which are not seen are eternal." 2 Corinthians 4:18. The exchange we make in the denial of selfish desires and inclinations is an exchange of the worthless and transitory for the precious and enduring. This is not sacrifice, but infinite gain.

"Something better" is the watchword of education, the law of all true living. Whatever Christ asks us to renounce, He offers in its stead something better. Often the youth cherish objects, pursuits, and pleasures that may not appear to be evil, but that fall short of the highest good. They divert the life from its noblest aim. Arbitrary measures or direct denunciation may not avail in leading these youth to relinquish that which they hold dear. Let them be directed to something better than display, ambition, or self-indulgence. Bring them in contact with truer beauty, with loftier principles, and with nobler lives. Lead them to behold the One "altogether lovely." When once the gaze is fixed upon Him, the life finds its center. The enthusiasm, the generous devotion, the passionate ardor, of the youth find here their true object. Duty becomes a delight and sacrifice a pleasure. To honor Christ, to become like Him, to work for Him, is the life's highest ambition and its greatest joy.

"The love of Christ constraineth." 2 Corinthians 5:14.

The Higher Course

"Since the beginning of the world men have not . . . perceived by the ear, neither hath the eyes see, . . . what He hath prepared for him that waiteth for Him."

35
The School of the Hereafter

"They shall see His face; and His name shall be in their foreheads."

Heaven is a school; its field of study, the universe; its teacher, the Infinite One. A branch of this school was established in Eden; and, the plan of redemption accomplished, education will again be taken up in the Eden school.

"Eye hath not seen, nor ear heard, neither have entered into the heart of man, the things which God hath prepared for them that love Him." 1 Corinthians 2:9. Only through His word can a knowledge of these things be gained; and even this affords but a partial revelation.

The prophet of Patmos thus describes the location of the school of the hereafter:

"I saw a new heaven and a new earth: for the first heaven and the first earth were passed away. . . . And I John saw the Holy City, New Jerusalem, coming down from God out of heaven, prepared as a bride adorned for her husband." Revelation 21:1, 2.

"The city had no need of the sun, neither of the moon, to shine in it: for the glory of God did lighten it, and the Lamb is the light thereof." Revelation 21:23.

Between the school established in Eden at the beginning and the school of the hereafter there lies the whole compass of this world's history—the history of human transgression and suffering, of divine sacrifice, and of victory over death and sin. Not all the conditions of that first school of Eden will be found in the school of the future life. No tree of knowledge of good and evil will afford opportunity for temptation. No tempter is there, no possibility of wrong. Every character has withstood the testing of evil, and none are longer susceptible to its power.

"To him that overcometh," Christ says, "will I give to eat of the tree of life, which is in the midst of the Paradise of God." Revelation 2:7. The giving of the tree of life in Eden was conditional, and it was finally withdrawn. But the gifts of the future life are absolute and eternal.

The prophet beholds the "river of water of life, clear as crystal, proceeding out of the throne of God and of the Lamb." "And on this side of the river and on that was the tree of life." "And there shall be no more death, neither sorrow, nor crying, neither shall there be any more pain: for the former things are passed away." Revelation 22:1; 22:2, R.V.; 21:4.

"Thy people also shall be all righteous:
They shall inherit the land forever,
    The branch of My planting,

The work of My hands,
That I may be glorified."

Isaiah 60:21.

Restored to His presence, man will again, as at the beginning, be taught of God: "My people shall know My name: . . . they shall know in that day that I am He that doth speak: behold, it is I." Isaiah 52:6.

"The tabernacle of God is with men, and He will dwell with them, and they shall be His people, and God Himself shall be with them, and be their God." Revelation 21:3.

"These are they which came out of great tribulation, and have washed their robes, and made them white in the blood of the Lamb. Therefore are they before the throne of God, and serve Him day and night in His temple. . . . They shall hunger no more, neither thirst any more; neither shall the sun light on them, nor any heat. For the Lamb which is in the midst of the throne shall feed them, and shall lead them unto living fountains of waters." Revelation 7:14-17.

"Now we see through a glass, darkly; but then face to face:" now we know in part; but then shall we know even as also we are known. 1 Corinthians 13:12.

"They shall see His face; and His name shall be in their foreheads." Revelation 22:4.

There, when the veil that darkens our vision shall be removed, and our eyes shall behold that world of beauty of which we now catch glimpses through the microscope; when we look on the glories of the heavens, now scanned afar through the telescope; when, the blight of sin removed, the whole earth shall appear in "the beauty of the Lord our God," what a field will be open to our study! There the student of science may read the records of creation and discern no reminders of the law of evil. He may listen to the music of nature's voices and detect no note of wailing or undertone of sorrow. In all created things he may trace one handwriting—in the vast universe behold "God's name writ large," and not in earth or sea or sky one sign of ill remaining.

There the Eden life will be lived, the life in garden and field. "They shall build houses, and inhabit them; and they shall plant vineyards, and eat the fruit of them. They shall not build, and another inhabit; they shall not plant, and another eat: for as the days of a tree are the days of My people, and Mine elect shall long enjoy the work of their hands." Isaiah 65:21, 22.

There shall be nothing to "hurt nor destroy in all My holy mountain, saith the Lord." Isaiah 65:25. There man will be restored to his lost kingship, and the lower order of beings will again recognize his sway; the fierce will become gentle, and the timid trustful.

There will be open to the student, history of infinite scope and of wealth inexpressible. Here, from the vantage ground of God's word, the student is afforded a view of the vast field of history and may gain some knowledge of the principles that govern the course of human events. But his vision is still clouded, and his knowledge incomplete. Not until he stands in the light of eternity will he see all things clearly.

Then will be opened before him the course of the great conflict that had its birth before time began, and that ends only when time shall cease. The history of the inception of sin; of fatal falsehood in its crooked working; of truth that, swerving not from its own straight lines, has met and conquered error—all will be made manifest. The veil that interposes between the visible and the invisible world will be drawn aside, and wonderful things will be revealed.

Not until the providences of God are seen in the light of eternity shall we understand what we owe to the care and interposition of His angels. Celestial beings have taken an active part in the affairs of men. They have appeared in garments that shone as the lightning; they have come as men, in the garb of wayfarers. They have accepted the hospitalities of human homes; they have acted as guides to benighted travelers. They have thwarted the spoiler's purpose and turned aside the stroke of the destroyer.

Though the rulers of this world know it not, yet often in their councils angels have been spokesmen. Human eyes have looked upon them. Human ears have listened to their appeals. In the council hall the court of justice, heavenly messengers have pleaded the cause of the persecuted and oppressed. They have defeated purposes and arrested evils that would have brought wrong and suffering to God's children. To the students in the heavenly school, all this will be unfolded.

Every redeemed one will understand the ministry of angels in his own life. The angel who was his guardian from his earliest moment; the angel who watched his steps, and covered his head in the day of peril; the angel who was with him in the valley of the shadow of death, who marked his resting place, who was the first to greet him in the resurrection morning—what will it be to hold converse with him, and to learn the history of divine interposition in the individual life, of heavenly co-operation in every work for humanity!

All the perplexities of life's experience will then be made plain. Where to us have appeared only confusion and disappointment, broken purposes and thwarted plans, will be seen a grand, overruling, victorious purpose, a divine harmony.

There all who have wrought with unselfish spirit will behold the fruit of their labors. The outworking of every right principle and noble deed will be seen. Something of this we see here. But how little of the result of the world's noblest work is in this life manifest to the doer! How many toil unselfishly and unweariedly for those who pass beyond their reach and knowledge! Parents and teachers lie down in their last sleep, their lifework seeming to have been wrought in vain; they know not that their faithfulness has unsealed springs of blessing that can never cease to flow; only by faith they see the children they have trained become a benediction and an inspiration to their fellow men, and the influence repeat itself a thousandfold. Many a worker sends out into the world messages of strength and hope and courage, words that carry blessing to hearts in every land; but of the results he, toiling in loneliness and obscurity, knows little. So gifts are bestowed, burdens are borne, labor is done. Men sow the seed from which, above their graves, others reap blessed harvests. They plant trees, that others may eat the fruit. They are content here to know that they have set in motion agencies for good. In the hereafter the action and reaction of all these will be seen.

Of every gift that God has bestowed, leading men to unselfish effort, a record is kept in heaven. To trace this in its wide-spreading lines, to look upon those who by our efforts have been uplifted and ennobled, to behold in their history the outworking of true principles—this will be one of the studies and rewards of the heavenly school.

There we shall know even as also we are known. There the loves and sympathies that God has planted in the soul will find truest and sweetest exercise. The pure communion with holy beings, the harmonious social life with the blessed angels and with the faithful ones of all ages, the sacred fellowship that binds together "the whole family in heaven and earth"—all are among the experiences of the hereafter.

There will be music there, and song, such music and song as, save in the visions of God, no mortal ear has heard or mind conceived.

"As well the singers as the players on instruments shall be there." Psalm 87:7. "They shall lift up their voice, they shall sing for the majesty of the Lord." Isaiah 24:14.

"For the Lord shall comfort Zion: He will comfort all her waste places; and He will make her wilderness like Eden, and her desert like the garden of the Lord; joy and gladness shall be found therein, thanksgiving, and the voice of melody." Isaiah 51:3.

There every power will be developed, every capability increased. The grandest enterprises will be carried forward, the loftiest aspirations will be reached, the highest ambitions realized. And still there will arise new heights to surmount, new wonders to admire, new truths to comprehend, fresh objects to call forth the powers of body and mind and soul.

All the treasures of the universe will be open to the study of God's children. With unutterable delight we shall enter into the joy and the wisdom of unfallen beings. We shall share the treasures gained through ages upon ages spent in contemplation of God's handiwork. And the years of eternity, as they roll, will continue to bring more glorious revelations. "Exceeding abundantly above all that we ask or think" (Ephesians 3:20) will be, forever and forever, the impartation of the gifts of God.

"His servants shall serve Him." Revelation 22:3. The life on earth is the beginning of the life in heaven; education on earth is an initiation into the principles of heaven; the lifework here is a training for the lifework there. What we now are, in character and holy service, is the sure foreshadowing of what we shall be.

"The Son of man came not to be ministered unto, but to minister." Matthew 20:28. Christ's work below is His work above, and our reward for working with Him in this world will be the greater power and wider privilege of working with Him in the world to come.

"Ye are My witnesses, saith the Lord, that I am God." Isaiah 43:12. This also we shall be in eternity.

For what was the great controversy permitted to continue throughout the ages? Why was it that Satan's existence was not cut short at the outset of his rebellion? It was that the universe might be convinced of God's justice in His dealing with evil; that sin might receive eternal condemnation. In the plan of redemption there are heights and depths that eternity itself can never exhaust, marvels into which the angels desire to look. The redeemed only, of all created beings, have in their own experience known the actual conflict with sin; they have wrought with Christ, and, as even the angels could not do, have entered into the fellowship of His sufferings; will they have no testimony as to the science of redemption—nothing that will be of worth to unfallen beings?

Even now, "unto the principalities and the powers in the heavenly places" is "made known through the church the manifold wisdom of God." And He "hath raised us up together, and made us sit together in heavenly places: . . . that in the ages to come He might show the exceeding riches of His grace in His kindness toward us through Christ Jesus." Ephesians 3:10, R.V.; 2:6, 7.

"In His temple doth everyone speak of His glory" (Psalm 29:9), and the song which the ransomed ones will sing—the song of their experience—will declare the glory of God: "Great and marvelous are Thy works, O Lord God, the Almighty; righteous and true are Thy ways, Thou King of the ages. Who shall not fear, O Lord, and glorify Thy name? for Thou only art holy." Revelation 15:3, 4, R.V.

In our life here, earthly, sin-restricted though it is, the greatest joy and the highest education are in service. And in the future state, untrammeled by the limitations of sinful humanity, it is in service that our greatest joy and our highest education will be found—witnessing, and ever as we witness learning anew "the riches of the glory of this mystery;" "which is Christ in you, the hope of glory." Colossians 1:27.

"It doth not yet appear what we shall be: but we know that, when He shall appear, we shall be like Him; for we shall see Him as He is." 1 John 3:2.

Then, in the results of His work, Christ will behold its recompense. In that great multitude which no man could number, presented "faultless before the presence of His glory with exceeding joy" (Jude 24), He whose blood has redeemed and whose life has taught us, "shall see of the travail of His soul, and shall be satisfied." Isaiah 53:11.

Index to Scripture References

Jeremiah

Ezekiel

Daniel

Hosea

Joel

Amos

Micah

Nahum

Habakkuk

Zephaniah

Haggai

Zechariah

Malachi

Matthew

Mark

Luke

John

Acts

Romans

1 Corinthians

2 Corinthians

Galatians

Ephesians

Philippians

Colossians

1 Thessalonians

2 Thessalonians

1 Timothy

2 Timothy

Hebrews

James

1 Peter

1 John

Jude

Revelation